The World of Moss
Illustrated guide book of Moss Terrariums and Gardening
By
Yoshihiro Ohno

苔の本 II

長く楽しむコケリウムの作り方。世界の美しい苔も探訪。

大野好弘

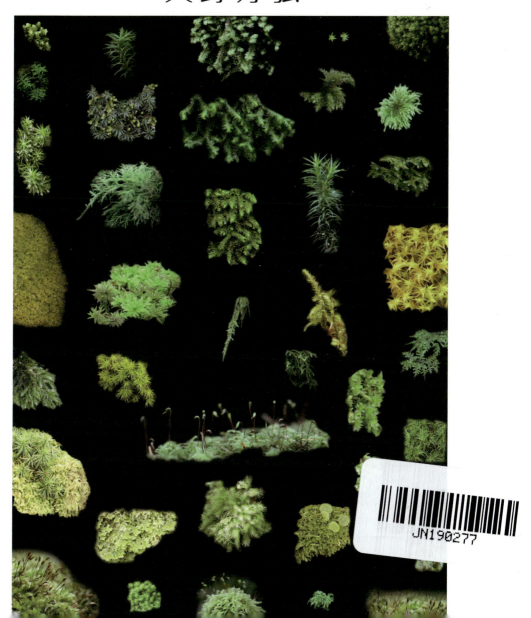

苔とコケリウムの世界へ。

　コケリウムとは苔を主体にアレンジしたテラリウムの一つです。

　この本の作品はすべてコケリウムです。

　苔を森の中で撮影し拡大して見ると、形や色の違いに驚かされます。

　苔に触れてみたり、香りを嗅いだり、五感で楽しむと、いっそう苔に惹かれます。

　そんな美しい苔を、身近に飾り眺めることで、心が落ち着き癒されるでしょう。

　この本では、苔を簡単に、しかも長く栽培できるヒントや、いろいろなコケリウムのアレンジ・作り方を紹介します。

　また、苔図鑑のなかでは、作る作品によっての最適なコケの種類を紹介しています。

　今日から、道端や森で苔の誘いに目を向けてみましょう。苔の美しさ、たっぷりの一冊です。

Introduction of Moss and Moss Gardening

Moss Terrarium is one of the way to design terrariums. In this book I introduce the unique designs of moss terrariums with photos and my own techniques.
When I take photos of mosses in the woods, I am always surprised by all of the different kinds. The touch and fragrant smells charm me even more. The beauty of moss can give you a world of tranquility and provide a peaceful atmosphere.

This book was created to introduce the secrets of growing moss long term and to show you the fascination and enchantment of mosses. In this book, you will find the most suitable moss for whatever kind of terrarium you may hope to make. I invite you to take a closer look at moss in your daily life.

P2 イギリス シルバーデールにて撮影。
P2 photo was taken in Silverdale. UK

苔とコケリウムの世界へ

目次

苔の美しさを求めて	7
イギリス	8
スロベニア	16
イタリア	19
クロアチア	22
ボスニア・ヘルツゴビナ	25
日本	
京都	26
群馬	36
金沢 兼六園	40
コラム1 苔の手入れ	43
北海道 松前	44
石川 来迎寺	46
苔図鑑	47
コケリウム用	48
アクアリウム・アクアテラリウム用	64
苔庭用	72
ヨーロッパのコケ	74
パルダリウム	82
コケリウムアレンジ	83
How to	119
コラム2 普通植物図譜	146
苔とは	147
苔の分類と体のしくみ	148
苔のライフサイクル	150
苔のこと	152
コラム3 カルチャースクール	152
Q&A	153
苔管理・作業	154
苔の生産	154
苔が見られる場所	155
良質な苔の販売ガイド	155
索引	156
あとがき	158
著者紹介	160
奥付け	160

The World of Moss and Moss Terrariums

Contents

Seeking After the Beautiful Moss	P7
United Kingdom	P8
Slovenia	P16
Italy	P19
Cloatia	P22
Bosnia-Herzegovina	P25
Japan	
Kyoto	P26
Gunma	P36
Kanazawa Kenrokuen	P40
Column1 Maintenance of Mosses	P43
Hokkaido Matumae	P45
Ishikawa Raikoji	P46
Illustrated Guide Book of Mosses	P47
For Moss Terrarium	P48
For Aquarium & Aqua Terrarium	P64
For Moss Gardens	P72
Guidebook of European Moss	P74
Paludarium	P82
Beautiful Collection of Moss Terrarium	P83
How to	P119
Column 2 A Pictorial Book of General Plants	P146
What is Moss?	P147
Classification of Mosses and the Body Structure	P148
Life Cycle of Moss	P150
About Mosses	P152
Column 3 Culture Schools	P152
Q&A	P153
Management task	P154
How to produce mosses	P154
Places where you can see mosses	P155
Good Quality Moss Shop Guide	P155
Index	P156
Postscript	P158
Auther's Profile	P160
Colophone	P160

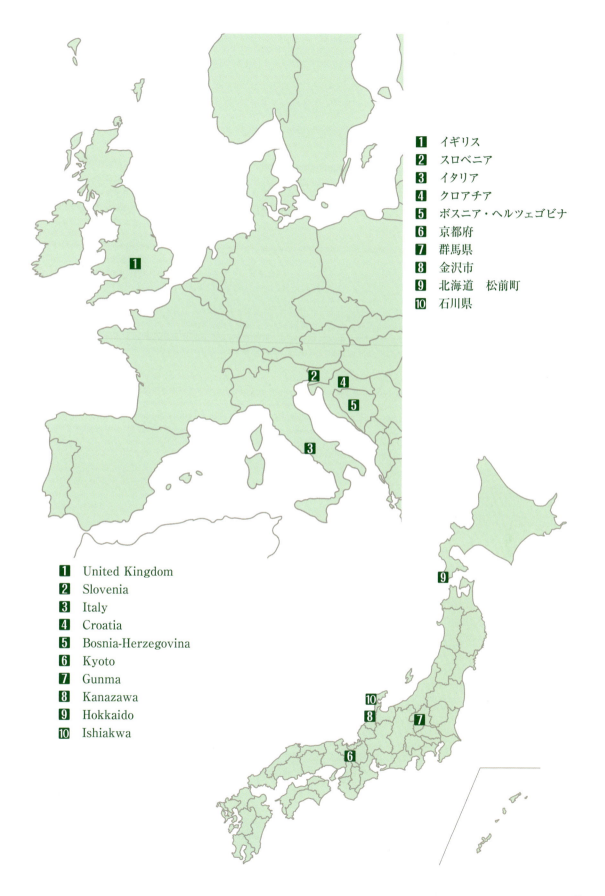

苔の美しさを求めて

　コケは世界に20,000種ほどあります。これらのコケは自生地によりいろいろな姿になります。年間を通して湿度が高い場所ではコケはずっと成長できるので大きく、またあまり雨が降らない場所や岩場ではあまり成長できないため背の低い小さなコケが生えています。とくにヨーロッパはコケにとって気温と湿度が適した地域です。
　ヨーロッパのコケの自生地と、日本のコケの美しい場所をご紹介します。

Seeking After the Beauty of Moss

There are 20,000 species of moss in the world. In humid conditions, the moss tends to grow bigger because it grows all year. On the contrary, in dry places or on rocks, the moss can't vegetate vigorously; therefore the moss is usually very small. Europe is the ideal place for mosses because of the temperature and humidity. I will introduce you to some places in Europe where you can observe the beauty of moss.

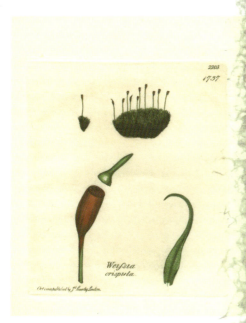

Weisia crispyla　1810年ジェームズ・サワビー

United Kingdom

イギリス

ビダルフ グランジ ガーデン

　イギリスには たくさんのガーデンがあります。この北イングランドにあるビダルフ グランジ ガーデンもその1つです。

　このガーデンは、19世紀後半に、ジェームス ベイトマン夫妻がこの地を購入し造られました。ガーデン内には朱色に塗られた回廊のある中国ガーデンや、背の低い生垣が綺麗なイタリアガーデン、スフィンクスの石像があるエジプトガーデンなどいろいろな国をイメージして造られたガーデンがあります。

　また150年近く前に集められた植物のなかに、モンキーパズルツリーもあり、今では林のようになっています。

　もちろん、植物やガーデンも素晴らしいですが、このガーデンはいろいろなところにたくさんの種類のコケが自生しており、観察できるのでお勧めです。

United Kingdom

Biddulph Grange Garden

There are so many beautiful gardens in the United Kingdom, but one of my favorites is Biddulph Grange Garden located in Northern England. This garden was first started in the 19th century by James & Mary Bateman, who collected plants from around the world. Today this world of gardens has a Chinese garden with red painted corridors displaying a hint of China, beautiful hedges in the Italian garden, and a stature of sphinx in the Egyptian garden. Also, about 150 years ago they planted huge monkey puzzle trees that have now become like a small forest. Apart from all these attractions of the gardens, you can also observe mosses in many places. I recommend taking a look at the English native mosses.

United Kingdom

シルバーデール

　イギリス北部にシルバーデールはあります。その小さな町には素敵な教会や、海岸線の夕日が綺麗なライムストーンでできた丘があります。シルバーデールには、ライムストーンを積み上げて作った、石垣で囲まれているヒツジの牧場がたくさんあります。その石垣にはたくさんの種類のコケやセダムの仲間、シダ植物が生えています。
　また、町のなかにも自然保護地域があり、イングリッシュブルーベル、ワイルドガーリック、プリムローズ、ワイルドナルシスなどが自生しています。保護地域の小道を歩き、コケや自然観察すると素敵な出会いがあるかもしれません。枯れ枝にラフストークトゥフェザーモスがクリスマスツリーのような可愛い姿を見せてくれました。

United Kingdom

Silverdale Lancashire

In Northern England, there is a lovely old town called Silverdale that has a beautiful limestone hill where you can see the sun setting over the coastline. There are also many pastures of sheep near limestone walls. On these walls, you can see many mosses, ferns, and sedums. The town has naturally reserved this area where English bluebells, wild garlic, primroses, and wild narcissus flourish. Why don't you take a stroll through this little lane? I discovered that the Ruff stalk feathers the moss on the dead branches, and makes it look like a Christmas decoration.

11

United Kingdom

ゲートバローズ

　シルバーデールの近くにゲートバローズはあります。ゲートバローズはライムストーンの石切り場でした。今は自然保護地域になって散策路が整備されています。ゲートを入ってすぐ足元や周りはすべて、シルバーグレーのライムストーンです。そのライムストーンはまるで氷河のクレパスのように隙間があります。この隙間には自然の岩付けといった感じに、コケやシダ、スゲが生えています。道を進むと昔の石切場の跡があります。苔むした切られたままのライムストーンが並んでます。崩れたラピュタ城のように。

　春にはコケの中からイングリッシュブルーベルが咲き、あたり一面、紫色の絨毯になるそうです。

United Kingdom

Gait Barrows Lancashire
Gait Barrows is located near Silverdale, and it used to be a quarry. As you take a stroll through this area, you will see the outstanding natural beauty of the typical limestone landscape that is well kept by the natural reserve. When you enter the gate, you will see silver-gray limestone that resembles the crevice of a glacier. Inside, you will find the natural rock covering of mosses, ferns, and sedges. Along the lanes, you will see the old quarry and which looks like a model of the Japanese animation movie "Castle in the Sky". In the spring, you may find the bluebells covering the fields like a blue carpet.

13

United Kingdom

ニュービーブリッジ

　湖水地方は湖がたくさんあり有名ですが、その周りにある小高い丘のような山も素敵です。この山の1つにニュービーブリッジの森があります。森の中の道は幅も広くなだらかなため、コケを観察しながら歩くのには最適です。そこにはコケの生えている根張りの凄い大きなオークがあります。ゆっくりコケの観察をしながら森林浴を楽しみましょう。

Newby Bridge - Lake District

The Lake District is very famous for the many beautiful lakes, mountains, and hills. The woodland walk of Newby Bridge has wide and gentle slopes suitable for observing mosses. You can find huge oak trees with big roots covered with moss. If you go in this area, please take your time to enjoy the therapeutic walk in the forest !

United Kingdom

ブラントウッド邸

　湖水地方のコニストン湖の側に、ブラントウッド邸はあります。この邸宅を1871年にジョン・ラスキン氏が購入し、250エーカーもある敷地に植林や沢を作り、まるで自然の森のような庭を造りました。この庭のなかには有名な、石版を重ね作られた椅子"ラスキンズチェアー"があります。石の表面にコケを纏い、素敵な姿になっています。

Brantwood - Lake District

Located by Lake Coniston, Brantwood was bought in 1871 by the author John Ruskin, who helped create the picturesque 250 acres of gardens. He planted woodland and created a valley. You will also see Ruskin's famous Chair, which was made by accumulated stone plates, and is now covered by mosses that leave you with a nostalgic feeling about the author.

15

Slovenia

スロベニア

　4月のスロベニアはまだ、たくさんの雪があります。標高2000mほどの高山では雪の中から、ヘレボルス・ニゲルの変異集団で、通称ピンクニゲルと呼ばれている花色がピンク色のタイプの花が急斜面に咲いていました。そして、少し降りたあたりの標高1700mの針葉樹の森には雪割草の仲間のヘパティカ・ノビリスが可憐なラベンダー色の花を咲かせていました。このあたりの岩はゴツゴツとしてその表面にはコケがたくさん生えていました。

Slovenia

In April, you will find lots of snow in Slovenia. On the steep slopes 2000 meters high on a mountain, I saw pink *Helleborus niger* flowers (Also known as Pink Niger). When I went down to 1700 meters, I found the *Hepatica nobilis* flowering with elegant lavender colors in the coniferous forest, as well as mosses on the surface of rugged rocks.

イタリア

　イタリアは、海岸線に出ればマテ貝やムール貝など魚介類が美味しく、またパスタもいろいろな種類があり楽しい国です。有名な観光スポットもたくさんあります。ピサの斜塔やベネツィア、フィレンツェなど魅力的な場所がいくつもありますが、山もまた素晴らしいです。手付かずの自然が豊かにあります。ヘレボルスやシクラメン、ヘパティカ、ガランサス、クロッカスなどの原種が間近で観察できます。また、岩にはいろいろな種類のコケが生え、写真を撮影するだけでも楽しいです。そんな森で、もしかしたら、苔仙人に出会えるかもしれませんね。

Italy

Italy is famous for the cuisine of seafood on the coastline, and of course, pasta as well. The scenic and tourist attractions are too numerous to count, like the leaning tower of Pisa, the lagoon city of Venice, the Renaissance city of Florence, and much more. However, I would like to introduce the mountains of Italy, where you can observe the original species of Helleborus, Cyclamen, Hepatica, Galanthus, Cruccusses, etc. Of course you can view the various mosses on the rocks, and I thoroughly enjoyed taking photos of them.

Italy

イタリア
　ヘパティカ・ノビリスを観察していると何か、視線を感じました。誰もいないはずの森なのにと思いながら、ふと見上げるとそこには苔の仙人が私を見ていました。自然のなす芸術に感動のあまり、涙が溢れてきました。

Italy
When I look at *Hepatica nobilis*, I feel like someone is watching and I am deeply touched by the natural art of it's creator.

イタリア

　標高1000m前後の林にはヘパティカ・ノビリスが自生しています。イタリアのある一か所ではピンク色や白などがありましたが、多くはラベンダー色の花です。花色の濃淡のほか、葉が真っ黒の個体もあり、たくさんの変異を観察できました。

Italy

In Italy, *Hepatica nobilis* grows naturally in the altitude of 1000 meters. Some places bloom with pink and white flowers, but it is mostly dominated by lavender colored flowers. I also found other flowers with blackish leaves.

クロアチア

　クロアチアは植物の宝庫です。町の広場には野草のお花畑があり、川沿いの道を少し入ればヘレボルスやヘパティカ、プリムローズ、アジュガが咲いていました。
　そんなクロアチアですが、日本では植物よりアニメの聖地として知られているかもしれません。海岸線に赤い屋根が連なる情景が描かれた魔女のアニメ。町を歩いていたら出会えるかも、と思ってしまうほど綺麗な街並みでした。
　町のすぐそばには標高の高い山がたくさんあります。石灰岩でできた山が多く、岩の表面にはコケがたくさん生えていました。白い石灰岩とコケの緑色とのコントラストが鮮やかで綺麗でした。木の根元に巻き付きながら生えているコケや、岩に着いている丸い球状のコケも観察できました。

Croatia

Croatia is the treasure box of plants. In town squares, you will find beds of wild flowers, and as you walk along the riverbanks, you can find helleborus, hepaticas, primroses and ajugas. In Japan, Croatia is famous for being the model town of animation films, because the country is well-kept and beautiful. There are also high mountains made of limestone, and these surfaces are covered by moss. The contrast of green moss and white limestone creates vivid and lovely scenery. Take a look at some of the mosses surrounding the bottoms of trees and the spherical mosses on rocks.

Croatia

Croatia

Bosnia-Herzegovina

ボスニア・ヘルツェゴビナ

　ボスニア・ヘルツゴビナからクロアチアの国境を目指し、山越えをしました。途中、片側が崖のような悪路が続きました。標高1600m近い尾根筋には、雪と苔の共演が見られました。また雪融けの脇にはスノードロップ（ガランサス）が咲いてました。正しく白く美しい雪の雫の妖精でした。

Bosnia-Herzegovina

We took the route from Bosnia-Herzegovina to the national border of Croatia, and the road along the cliff was not good, so be careful if you take this route. At 1600 meters high, you can observe the beautiful performance of snow and mosses on the ridge. As the snow melts, I found the pure white Snowdrops (Garanthus) flowering.

京都
東福寺

　東山区にある東福寺は鎌倉時代に建造されました。1939年重森三玲によって、東に北斗七星の庭、南に苔の築山で五山を表す蓬莱神仙思想の庭、西に井田市松の庭、北に小市松模様の庭の本坊庭園が造られました。

　この北に位置する小市松模様の庭は切石とウマスギゴケが規則正しく配置され非常に美しいものです。規則正しい配列はだんだんと切石が少なくなり最後は 州浜の形に切石がなくなっていきます。とくに雨の後は苔の緑が鮮やかに、また濡れた切石が白く、いっそう市松模様のコントラストが艶やかになります。

KYOTO
Tofukuji

Tofukuji was built in the Kamakura period, and in 1939 the famous garden designer, Mirei Shigemori, created the Big Dipper shaped garden in the east corner. The southern garden has artificial hills to help you imagine the five mountains of Arcadia. The checkered pattern garden in the north is designed with square stones and Polytrichum commune. The checkered pattern stones are set in line regularly, but it gradually changes and may eventually disappear. After the rain, the green moss is brilliantly enhanced with the whitish stones. It is one of the most beautiful modern Japanese gardens.

東福寺
Tofukuji

泉涌寺

　京都にはたくさんの寺院があります。お寺を訪ねてみると、お寺ごとにさまざまなコケのある庭が見られます。ふだん、渓流や深山に行かなければなかなか見ることのできないタマゴケも、お寺に行く参道にあり驚かされます。

　泉涌寺は東福寺と同じ東山区にあります。その泉涌寺に御座所庭園はあります。御座所庭園は明治17年に両陛下や皇族方の御休憩所として造られました。縁側からは池のある庭園が一望できます。この御座所庭園にある雪見灯篭は上京区にある仙洞御所から移築されました。

　庭園にはたくさんのモミジやツツジが植えられています。また一面がいろいろなコケで覆われ、そのグラデーションがとても綺麗です。

Sennyuji

There are many temples in Kyoto, where you will find various mosses. Sennyuji and Tohukuji are located in Higashiyama district. I was surprised to discover Bartramia pomifornis usually found in the deep mountains was on the way to the temple. Gozasyo garden was created in 1884, which is the place where the Royal family stopped to take a rest. The garden has many maple trees, azaleas, and mosses that create an amazing effect from the deep contrast of the plants.

Kyoto

高台寺

　高台寺は東山区に1606年、豊臣秀吉の妻の北政所ねねが、秀吉の菩提を弔うために開山したお寺です。
　寺内には小堀遠州作の池泉廻遊式庭園があります。庭園には11石の石組みの庭、湖月庵前庭、枯山水式の遺芳庵前庭、雲居庵前庭「竹風庭」、枯山水式の方文前庭「波心庭」があり、砂紋、白砂からなっています。
　春には西の州浜に植えてある桜色のシダレザクラが咲き彩りを加えます。砂の周りには州浜があり、コケが植えられています。初夏は青竹色の竹林が、秋には紅葉したモミジが、冬には美しい雪景色が見られます。

Kodaiji

Kodaiji was built in 1606 by the wife of Hideyosi to commemorate him because he was the famous ruler of Japan in the late 16th century. There is also a garden designed by Ensyu Kobori, who was one of the most famous garden designers in the 17th century. Some of his designs are the Stone garden, Kogetuan front garden. The dry garden called "Hasintei" consists of only white sand. At the Suhama (sandy beach) you will find pink, weeping cherry flowers, as well as planted moss. Each season displays the unique beauty of Japan.

常寂光寺

　嵐山は、春はサクラ、秋はモミジと美しく、渡月橋や嵯峨野の竹林があります。
　その竹林を抜けた先の小倉山の中腹に常寂光寺はあります。お寺は斜面にあり、周りにはモミジが200本ほど植えられていて、秋には真っ赤に染まります。
　頂上近くには重要文化財の多宝塔があり、そこまでは苔むした石の階段を歩きます。階段の周りには苔の海が広がり、陽が差し込むと葉先がキラキラ輝いて見えます。また季節によっていろいろな山野草の花を観察できます。

Jojakkoji

Arashiyama is the lovely countryside in Kyoto, where you can find cherry blossoms in the spring, and leaves of maple trees and bamboo forests of Togetukyo and Sagano in the autumn. Jojakkoji is located in the middle of Ogura mountain and was built on the slope where you will find 200 maple trees. The slope turns into scarlet in the autumn. Near the top of the mountain, there is a pagoda of the important cultural property. When you go up there, you can step on the stone staircase covered with moss. A sea of moss is spread out along the side of the staircase as well. When the sun shines, the tip of the foliage looks like it is glittering. You can discover beautiful wild flowers in every season.

Kyoto

祇王寺

　嵐山の奥、嵯峨の地に祇王寺はあります。周りは緑鮮やかな竹林に囲まれています。

　祇王寺は平家物語にも登場する尼寺です。寺内にはたくさんのモミジが植えられ、細い小川が流れています。この小川のほとりには緑色のオオスギゴケ、その周り一帯には黄緑色のヒノキゴケが一面に広がります。生え揃ったヒノキゴケの姿は圧巻です。

　回廊の途中には祇王寺に生えているコケの展示もあります。その先には草庵があり、周りには透き通る緑色のコツボゴケが瑞々しい姿を見せてくれます。静かな時の流れのなか、ゆっくりと苔を楽しむことのできるお庭です。

Giouji

In a hidden area of Arashiyama, there is a place called Saga where you will find Giouji. There is an ancient convent, mentioned in " Heike Monogatari" (Old History Book of Taira family), that is surrounded by a lush, green, bamboo forest, maple trees and a brook. Along the stream, you can see green *Polytrichum commune* surrounded by yellow-green *Pymrrhobryum dozyanum*, which creates outstanding scenery. On the way to the corridor, they exhibit moss of Giouji. There is a hut surrounded by the transparent green *Plagiomnim acutum*. This is a garden where you can enjoy the tranquility and stillness of observing mosses as long as you want.

群馬
チャツボミゴケ公園

　群馬県の中之条町にあるチャツボミゴケ公園には、酸性の温泉に生えるチャツボミゴケ、学名ユンゲルマンニア・ブルカニコーラの国内で最大規模の群落があります。

　5月にはチャツボミゴケの生えている周りにオレンジ色のレンゲツツジが咲き、初夏には道の周りにヨツバヒヨドリが咲き、アサギマダラの楽園になります。また、秋にはモミジがたくさんあるので、真っ赤に紅葉した葉とチャツボミゴケの緑が重なり見事な景色になります。チャツボミゴケの自生地、穴地獄の左手にある小高い丘では、シラタマノキ、アカモノ、スノキ、ガンコウラン、ヤマオダマキなどが観察できます。

　この群落には温泉のほかに沢の水も流れ込んでいます。右手ルートで観察を続けると、沢の水と温泉のお湯とが混ざり合う場所があり、温泉水にはチャツボミゴケ、沢の水にはコツボゴケやシッポゴケが生え住み分けています。

　色の違いですぐ見分けられます。群落地には木道が整備されていて、じっくり観察できます。

Gunma
Chatsubomigoke Park

Chatsubomigoke Park is located in Nakanojo in the Gunma region, where one of the largest colonies of *Jungermannia vulcanicola* grows alongside the stream of an Acidic spring. It is beautiful in May when the orange flowers of *Rhododendron japonicum* open around the moss. In early summer, when *Eupatorium glehnii* blooms, the place turns into a paradise of chestnut tiger butterflies (*Parantica sita*). In autumn, red-colored maple leaves cover the lush, green moss. On the hillside of Anajigoku, you may find *Gaultheria, G.adenothrix. Vaccinium, Empetrum nigrum,* and *Aquillegia buergeriana*. There is a place where two streams meet together, and you can see *Jungermannia vulcanicola* on the side of the hot spring, and *Plagiomnium acutum* and *Dicranum japonicum* on the side of the cold stream. You can easily identify the difference from the color of the moss.

草津白根山

　チャツボミゴケ公園がある中之条町の近くに草津温泉があります。日本有数の人気温泉で、中心には湯の花を採取する湯畑があります。
　草津温泉は標高1200mの高山にあります。そのため、町を散策すればすぐにコイワカガミなどの高山植物に出会うことができます。また、草津温泉から志賀高原ルートを走り白根山のほうへ行く途中には、ツマトリソウ、アズマシャクナゲ、タカネザクラ(ミネザクラ)なども観察できます。

Kusatsu Shiranesan

Kusatsu hot spring is near Nakanojo, and it is one of the most popular hot springs in Japan. It is located in the altitude of 1200 meters high. As you walk in the area, you can find alpine plants like *Schizocodon soldanelloides*, as well as *Trientalis europaea, Rhodondendron degronianum,* and *Carasus nipponica* on the way to Shirane mountain from Shiga highland.

39

金沢
兼六園

　石川県金沢市に兼六園はあります。
　岡山の後楽園、水戸の偕楽園とともに日本三名園の一つです。 兼六園は1600年代から前田家が作庭し、1822年に兼六園と命名されました。
　兼六園という名は幽邃、人力、宏大、水泉、眺望、蒼古の6つの景勝を兼ね備えているという意味でつけられています。
　園内には根上松、唐崎松、姫子松、乙葉松、播州松などの、庭園には欠かせない見事なマツがあります。根上松の周りは一面綺麗な苔に覆われています。また、春にはウメやサクラが咲きます。園内にウメは200本、サクラは20種420本あり、なかには兼六園の名がついたケンロクエンフユザクラ(兼六園冬桜)やケンロクエンキクザクラ(兼六園菊桜)、ケンロクエンクマガイ(兼六園熊谷)などがあります。
　初夏にはカキツバタ、秋にはモミジ、冬の雪吊りが有名です。
　園内はどこを見ても苔が美しく、とくに山崎山の周辺の苔は、周りに小川や池があり湿度が高いため綺麗です。
　園内ではコバノチョウチンゴケ、ヤマトフデゴケ、ナミガタタチゴケ、ウマスギゴケ、ホソバオキナゴケ、ホソバミズゼニゴケなどが見られます。

Kanazawa
Kenrokuen

Kenrokuen is located in Kanazawa in the Ishikawa region. It is one of the three most famous Japanese gardens, together with Kourakuen in Okayama region and Kairakuen in Mito city. Kenrokuen was first created in the early 17th century and was developed by the successive generation of Lord Maeda. Kenrokuen literally means having the six virtues: mystery, human strength, grand scale, water, weathering, and perspective. There are many beautiful pine trees in the epitome of Japanese gardens. Neagarimatu is covered by beautiful mosses. Early spring first blooms Plum flowers, and then Cherry blossoms. There are 200 plum trees, also 420 cherry trees of many varieties, Kenrokuen kikuzakura, and Kenrokuen kumagai, Kenrokuen fuyuzakura are named after the garden itself. It is very famous for the winter protection of branches called Yukituri, (literally means snow hung) which provides a place the branches to hang on to during the winter. When the snow is thick and moist, it can easily damage the branches. You can also find *Trachycystis mocrophylla, Campylopus japonicas, Atrichum undulatum, Polytricum commune, Leucobryum juniperoideum,* and *Pellia endiviifolia*.

時雨亭

　兼六園内には三芳庵、時雨亭、奇観亭、ことぶき、兼六亭、内橋亭の6つの茶店があります。時雨亭は2000年に長谷池のほとりに、6代目藩主、前田吉徳が建てた茶室を再現した茶店です。季節の生和菓子と共に抹茶をいただくことができます。茶室からは長谷池や綺麗な苔の植えられている庭を眺めることができます。

Shiguretei

Shiguretei was built in 2000, and is a recreational Tea House made by 6th Lord Yoshinori Maeda. You can enjoy the seasonal, sweet, green powder tea and view the beautiful moss garden and hase pond.

苔の手入れ
Column ❶

苔のある庭園では、苔の手入れを怠ると苔はすぐに傷み、他の植物に駆逐されます。そのため、たくさんのガーデナーによって、苔の間に生えた草の除去や、落ち葉拾い、傷んだ苔の張り替えが行われて、綺麗な苔の庭園が保たれているのです。

Maintenance of mosses

It is necessary to maintain moss gardens, because they are easily damaged and driven out by other plants. Therefore, in many beautiful moss gardens, they have a lot of gardeners to keep out weeds, clean up dead leaves, and replace damaged mosses for healthy ones.

北海道 松前 法憧寺
Hokkaido Matumae Houdouji

北海道
松前 法憧寺 松前城

　北海道の渡島半島南西部にある松前町は、かつては松前藩の松前城城下町です。ウニやカニ、マグロなどの海産物が豊富で松前漬けは有名です。
　松前城がある松前公園には250種約1万本のサクラが植えられています。その多くは桜研究家の浅利政俊氏が手入れ管理されています。緑色の鬱金、大きな花を咲かせる太白、浅利氏が交配により作出したいろいろな八重咲き種などがあります。そして、近くには苔の綺麗なお寺、法憧寺があります。

Hokkaido
Matsumae Houdouji Matsumaejou

Matsumae is rich in marine products and is located on the Southwest part of the Oshima Peninsula. In Matsumae park, they planted 10,000 cherry trees of 250 different varieties. For example, a green-flowered cherries called Ukon and a bigger flowered Taihaku. Many of them are grown by the cherry breeder, Masatoshi Asari, who specializes in breeding and creating various double-flowered cherries. Houdouji is nearby, where you can also find beautiful mosses.

石川県 来迎寺

　石川県の鳳珠郡穴水町に来迎寺はあります。来迎寺の前身青龍寺は、814 年に中川実範大徳が建立しました。来迎寺は花の寺とも呼ばれています。お寺の中には八重咲きのツツジや、オオミスミソウ、ミズバショウなどたくさんの植物が植えられています。また、樹齢数百年の天然記念物のライコウジキクザクラがあります。キクザクラとはヤマザクラの子宝咲きで、ライコウジキクザクラは 200 枚以上の花弁がつきます。また、心字池のある来迎寺庭園があり、池の周りの石は苔むしていて、なんとも言えない風情があります。

Ishikawa Raikoji

Raikoji is called a temple of flowers and is located in Anamizu, Housugun. There are double flowered Azaleas, *Hepatica nobilis var. japonica f. magna*, *Lysichiton camtschatcensis*, and more. Raikoji kikuzakura was designated as a special natural treasure because it is several hundred years old and has more than 200 fine petals. Similar to the chrysanthemum, the Raikoji garden has a pond shaped in the Chinese character of a heart. The stones around the pond are covered with mosses. The whole atmosphere is very touching.

苔図鑑

コケリウム用
アクアリウム・アクアテラリウム用
苔庭用
ヨーロッパの苔図鑑

Illustrated Guide Book of Moss in Japan

For Moss Terrarium
For Aquarium & Aqua Terrarium
For Moss Gardens
Guidebook of European Moss

Grimmia apocarpa　1803年 ジェームズ・サワビー

苔図鑑のデータ

栽培難易度	✤	容易
	✤✤	ふつう
	✤✤✤	難しい
日当り・明るさ	✻	日陰を好む(あまり照明がない空間)
	✻✻	半日陰を好む(照明のある空間)
	✻✻✻	半日なたを好む(レースカーテンのある窓辺)
温度	✳	対暑性がない
	✳✳	中間
	✳✳✳	対暑性がある
湿度	💧	乾燥を好む
	💧💧	適度な湿り気を好む
	💧💧💧	濡れた状態を好む

Cultivation Guide of Mosses

Difficulty of cultivation	✤	Easy
	✤✤	Ordinary
	✤✤✤	Difficult
Light Intensity	✻	Shady place …(Place of very little illumination)
	✻✻	Half Shady place …(Place with illumination)
	✻✻✻	Half Sunny Place …(By the window with Lace curtain)
Temperature	✳	Intolerant of Hot Weather
	✳✳	Middle
	✳✳✳	Heat Torelance
Humidity	💧	Dryness
	💧💧	Moderate Humidity
	💧💧💧	Wet Condition

コケリウム用 　　　　　　　　　　　　　　　　　　　　　For Moss Terrarium

ウマスギゴケ

【馬杉苔】

明るいアカマツ林や避暑地、林道の脇や湿原に50cmほどの巨大なコロニーを作り生える。枝分かれはせず、1本ずつ単独で成長する。

葉は1cm位で放射状に付ける。環境が良いと高さ20cmほどまで伸びる。スギゴケ類では珍しく、中心まで緑色のままのものが多い。

苔庭で使われるスギゴケはほとんどがスギゴケではなく、ウマスギゴケとなる。

コケリウムなどでは、葉の間の落ち葉や、傷んだ箇所を取り除いてから用いるよい。仮根部が水没すると傷み枯れやすい。

スギゴケの仲間は乾燥するとすぐ葉を閉じるため、まめに霧吹きで水を与える。

日本全土、世界中ほとんどの場所に分布している。

Polytrichum commune

栽培難易度	Difficulty of cultivation
日当り・明るさ	Light Intensity
温度	Temperature
湿度	Humidity

Umasugigoke

It grows in the sparse red pine wood by the woodland road or marsh, and it is a single-stem plant with no branches. You can find the huge colony about 50cm wide with radial shaped leaves 1cm long. In the best conditions it grows 20cm high, and it is a rare example of cedar moss with green leaves in the center. It is used in nearly any Moss Garden. When making a moss terrarium, it is better to take off the damaged parts and do not put temporary roots in the water! This damages the plants and causes them to wither. However, you can spray water on them from time to time to prevent the leaves from shrinking. It is distributed in all of Japan and almost any countries in the world.

コケリウム用　　　　　　　　　　　　　　　　　　　　　For Moss Terrarium

エゾスナゴケ　　　　　　　　　　　　*Racomitrium japonicum*

【蝦夷砂苔】

栽培難易度	❖❖	Difficulty of cultivation
日当り・明るさ	☀☀☀	Light Intensity
温度	✳✳	Temperature
湿度	💧	Humidity

Ezosunagoke

　陽当たりが良く風通しも良い岩の表面や、砂地の草原、砂の堆積した道路脇に生える。環境が良いと5cmほどまで伸び、モップのようになる。

　乾燥すると葉は黄色で葉先は白くなり、モールのように縮れて捩れる。雨で濡れたり湿っていると葉は明るい黄緑色になる。濡れて葉が開いた姿は美しく、上から見るとお星様のようで可愛い。

　マット状に広がり繁殖するが、仮根はあまりつながらないため、1本ずつすぐにバラける。

　水を嫌うため、コケリウムでは水没しないように配置するか、底に孔を開けた容器を使うとよい。また、湿気を嫌うため、蓋のある容器での栽培は難しい。日本全土にあり、北半球に分布する。

It grows on the surface of rocks in sunny and airy sites, sandy grasslands or on the piles of sand by the roadside. When fully grown, it resembles a mop, and with the right conditions it can become 5cm high.
When it's dry, the leaves turn yellow and the leaf apex becomes whitish, curly and twisted. In the rain, the bright, yellow-green foliage is beautiful. When the leaves open, each one looks like a tiny and cute star. Although it propagates like a mat shape, the temporary roots are not really linked. So, it can easily be divided one by one. This moss doesn't like water and humidity, so do not submerge it in a terrarium. I recommend using containers without a lid that have a hole on the bottom. It is distributed in all of Japan and the Northern hemisphere.

コケリウム用　　　　　　　　　　　　　　　　　　　　　For Moss Terrarium

オオカサゴケ　　　　　　　　　　*Rhodobryum giganteum*

【大傘苔】

栽培難易度	✿✿	Difficulty of cultivation
日当り・明るさ	☀	Light Intensity
温度	✳	Temperature
湿度	●●	Humidity

Ookasagoke

日陰の常緑樹の下、落ち葉の積もる緩やかな斜面に小さな群落をつくる。葉が濡れて展開していないとわかりにくい。展開すると番傘を開いた姿に似る。長い地下茎でつながる。

高さは6～8cmで直立茎の先に1～2cmほどの濃緑色の長鱗片状の葉を放射状に付ける。日本海側には小形のカサゴケがある。

コケリウムでは蓋のある容器に用土を多めに入れ、地下茎を埋めて栽培するとよい。葉のある直立茎は、1年で枯れ、春に地下茎から新しく直立茎が伸び出る。

本州、四国、九州、沖縄に生える。また、中国、ハワイ。南アフリカ、マダガスカルにもある。

It inhabits as small communities underneath evergreen trees in the shade or on the calm slope of accumulated dead leaves. It is difficult to find unless an umbrella-like foliage opens up in wet conditions. Plants are connected to each other with long rhizomes. Dark green scale-like leaves of 1-2cm long develop radially on top of the 6-8cm upright stems. Smaller *R. roseum* exist on the coastline of the Sea of Japan.
In a terrarium, I put extra soil to bury rhizomes. The leaves wither in a year and new stems will emerge the next Spring. It is distributed in Japan except Hokkaido, China, Hawaii, South Africa, or Madagascar.

コケリウム用　　　　　　　　　　　　　　　　　　　　　　For Moss Terrarium

クジャクゴケ　　　　　　　　　　　　　　*Hypopterugium fauriei*

【孔雀苔】

栽培難易度	✿✿	Difficulty of cultivation
日当り・明るさ	☀☀	Light Intensity
温度	✳✳	Temperature
湿度	●●	Humidity

Kujakugoke

　日陰の湿った斜面、岩盤にまとまって生える。

　地下茎は枝分かれしつながる。直立茎から横に葉の付いた枝を扇状に付ける。乾燥すると開いていた枝が閉じ、葉の色が茶色に近くなる。高さは1〜2.5cm。葉は透明感のない茶緑色の卵型で長さ1.5㎜、扇状に広がった枝に付ける。クジャクが羽を開いた姿に似ているため、和名がクジャクゴケとされている。

　コケリウムでは蓋のある容器に入れて栽培するとよい。仮根の水没を嫌うため、水に浸からないように配置するとよい。

　本州、四国、九州に生える。また、中国、北米西部にもある。

It grows as a mass in the shady slope or bedrock, and Rhizomes branch out to connect.
The upright stems emerge as fan-shaped shoots with leaves. When it's dry, the fan will be closed and the color will turn brownish. It is 1-2.5cm high and the cloudy brownish-green leaves are egg-shaped and 1.5 mm wide. The shape of foliage is like a peacock with opened feathers. The common name is Kujakugoke, which means 'peacock moss' in Japanese. It is better to use a container with a lid, because the temporary roots do not like water. It is distributed in Honsyu, Sikoku, Kyusyu, China and Western North America.

コケリウム用　　　　　　　　　　　　　　　　　　　　For Moss Terrarium

コツボゴケ

【小壺苔】

Plagiomnium acutum

Kotsubogoke

栽培難易度		Difficulty of cultivation
日当り・明るさ		Light Intensity
温度		Temperature
湿度		Humidity

スギが多い林道の脇、水辺、つねに濡れている岩場の表面や、堆積物のある岩の上にマット状に生える。

葉は透明感のある緑色で、地面を這うように広がる。葉は卵形で先端が尖り、3㎜ほど。高さは2㎝ほどで横に広がる。コツボゴケの雌株は、緑色の小さな花が咲いたような姿になる。

非常に乾燥に弱いため、コケリウムでは蓋のある容器で栽培するか、水の溜まる器に、水が好きな他の植物といっしょに植えるとよい。湿度が少ないと葉の縁から白く縮れ枯れる。一度白くなると戻らない。

容器の中で栽培すると、葉はガラス細工のような透明感のある明るい緑色になる。日本全土、アジアに分布する。

You can find it by the roadside of cedar woodland, water, on the surface of wet rocks, or on rocks with sediment.
It covers like a mat and has translucent green leaves that are egg-shaped, pointed on the tip, and 3 mm. It spreads horizontally like crawling on the ground and is 2 cm high. Female plants look like they have tiny green flowers.
It is very vulnerable to dryness, so terrariums should have a lid or plant it in a water container mixing with other water-loving plants. When it becomes dry, the foliage turns whitish with curly edges, and it can never regain the greenness.
In glass, it becomes bright green. It is distributed all over Japan and Asia.

52

コケリウム用 / For Moss Terrarium

ヒノキゴケ

Trachycystis microphylla

【檜苔】

Hinokigoke

栽培難易度	Difficulty of cultivation
日当り・明るさ	Light Intensity
温度	Temperature
湿度	Humidity

明るい風通しの良い林の斜面に多い、10cmほどのコロニーが多いが、環境が合うと一面に広がり生える。ウマスギゴケなどが好む環境より、もう少し乾いた環境に多い。

茎は10cmほど。葉は透明感のない黄緑色の針状で10mmほど。密につく。葉が乾燥すると内側に巻き込み細くまとまる。見た目から別名イタチノシッポとも呼ばれる。

コケリウムでは蓋のない容器に栽培するとよい。仮根が水没すると枯れやすい。霧吹きで葉に水分を与えるとよい。他の植物との寄せ植えにも使いやすい。

本州、四国、九州、沖縄に生える。朝鮮、中国、インドネシアにもある。

It often occurs on the slopes of luminous and airy woodlands and develops colonies of 10 cm wide. Yet, sometimes they can spread all over. You can find them in drier conditions than *Politrichum commune*. (Umasugigoke)
They have 10 mm needle shaped yellow-green leaves with dense stems 10cm long. When it is dry, they shrink inward and become thin and tight. The common name is weasel's tail (Itachinoshippo in Japanese). It is better to cultivate it in a terrarium without a lid. Don't submerge temporary roots, but instead spray the leaves. It can be used as a group planting. It is distributed in Honshu, Shikoku, Kyusyu, Okinawa, Korea, China and Indonesia.

コケリウム用   For Moss Terrarium

シシゴケ   *Brothera leana*

【獅子苔】

栽培難易度	✤✤	Difficulty of cultivation
日当り・明るさ	☀☀☀	Light Intensity
温度	✱✱	Temperature
湿度	●	Humidity

Shishigoke

　日の当たる大木の根元や、山の岩の窪み、砂質の土の上に生える。光沢の強い緑色で、丸または長卵形のコロニーを作る。時に広範囲に広がり地面を覆う。

　針状の長さ1cmほどの葉を付ける。この種類は非常に成長が遅く、栽培下ではコロニーが倍の大きさになるのに3年ほど要する。葉が硬いため、乾燥してもあまり見た目が変わらない。濡れると光沢が増す。

　シシゴケはコケリウムにとって非常に使いやすい。とくに多肉植物やサボテンなどとのアレンジによい。

　水を嫌うため、蓋のない容器で乾かし気味に栽培する。湿った状態が続くと、表面や内部にクモノスカビが生え、やがて真っ黒になり枯れてしまう。

　分布域は北海道、本州、四国、九州、朝鮮、中国、アフリカ、北米。

It is a slow growing moss found on the base of large trees, in the cavities of rocks in the mountains, or in sandy soil. It's strong, glossy, green colonies become round or oval shaped, and sometimes spread out in wide spaces covering the ground. They have needle-shaped leaves that are 1 cm long. Under cultivation, it takes three years to double the size of the colony. Since the leaves are hard, it doesn't look much different when it is dry. But when it is wet, it looks glossy. It is easy and useful for moss terrarium gardening, and it especially matches well with succulent plants or cacti. Grow it in a container without a lid and keep it in dry conditions. If it stays in humidity for a long time, rhizopus (saprobic fungus) will grow and eventually kill the moss and turn it black.
It is distributed in Hokkaido, Honshu, Shikoku, Kyushu, Korea, China, Africa, and North America.

コケリウム用 / For Moss Terrarium

ジャゴケ　　　　　　　　　　　　　　　　　*Conocephalum conicum*

【蛇苔】　　　　　　　　　　　　　　　### Jagoke

栽培難易度	✦✦✦	Difficulty of cultivation
日当り・明るさ	☀	Light Intensity
温度	✱	Temperature
湿度	●●●	Humidity

涼しく水が滲み出る日陰の斜面、沢筋の水がかかる岩や湿り気のある斜面に生える。環境が良いと壁面全体を覆うように生える。葉状体は光沢のある鮮やかなエメラルドグリーン色で長さが10cmほどになる。見た目がヘビの鱗のように見えるところからジャゴケと和名が付いている。

葉状体の裏面から白い糸状の仮根が長く伸びる。個体により香りの違いや強さはあるが、コケでは珍しく葉を折ったり、すり潰すと、ミント系または柑橘系の爽やかな香りがする。

姿が変わっているため人気がありコケリウムにも使う。水が好きなため蓋の閉まる容器で栽培するとよい。

日本全土、北半球に広く分布する。

You can find it on shady slopes where cool water oozes out of the stream, by the sidewalks of mountains, where damp slopes splash water. In an ideal condition, it covers all the walls and has shiny, vivid, emerald-green foliage that is 10 cm long. The common Japanese name Jagoke was derived from snake scales, and resembles foliage. Temporary roots like white strings emerge from the backside of the leaves. It depends on the individual plants, but it usually smells like mint or citrus when you crush the leaves. This is unusual for moss. It is popular for moss terrarium arrangements, and the container should have a lid because it likes water. It is distributed in Japan and the Northern hemisphere.

コケリウム用　　　　　　　　　　　　　　　　　For Moss Terrarium

タマゴケ　　　　　　　　　　　　　*Bartramia pomiformis*

【玉苔】

栽培難易度	✤ ✤	Difficulty of cultivation
日当り・明るさ	✸ ✸	Light Intensity
温度	✱ ✱	Temperature
湿度	●	Humidity

Tamagoke

　湿度が高く直射日光が当たらない明るい崖、渓流添いの乾いた斜面に生える。時折ショウジョウバカマといっしょに生えている。

　7mmほどの細く尖った明るい緑色の針状の葉を放射状に付ける。茎の高さは5センチ前後。コロニー状の塊が多く、時に斜面を覆う。

　胞子は丸く初めは緑色。熟すと、中心から赤味を帯びる。丸い胞子は可愛く人気がある。

　コケリウムでは石に接着するか、なるべく上部に配置する。湿気は好きだが仮根が水に浸かることを嫌う。

　また、空気が流動するように蓋を半開きにして栽培するとよい。日本全土、北半球に分布する。

It prefers luminous but it is better without direct sunlight and high humidity. In the dry slopes along the mountain streams you can occasionally find with *Heloniopsis orientalis*.
It is 7 mm long, light green, and has fine-pointed needle-shaped leaves attached to the stems that are 5 cm long. It can be found as a colony and sometimes covering the slopes. Spores are round and green in the beginning, but once it matures it turns reddish in the center. It is cute and very popular.
In a container, it is better to adhere on stones or upper places, because temporary roots hate to submerge. Also, it is important to open the lid half way for ventilation. It is distributed to all of Japan and the Northern hemisphere.

コケリウム用　　　　　　　　　　　　　　　　　　　　For Moss Terrarium

トヤマシノブゴケ　　　　　　*Thuidium kanedae*

【外山忍苔】

栽培難易度	✿✿	Difficulty of cultivation
日当り・明るさ	☀☀	Light Intensity
温度	✱✱	Temperature
湿度	●●●	Humidity

Toyamashinobugoke

藪の脇、山地の半日陰の斜面、岩の表面などにマット状に生える。日当りの違いで葉の色が黄緑色から濃緑色になる。水に浸かるような場所でも生育する。

茎の長さは15cmほどで葉は細かく1mmほどで茎にびっしりつく。

和名は姿がシダ植物のシノブに似ているため。葉は濡れていると緑色。冬季には黄金色に紅葉する。葉が乾燥するとすぐに縮れる。

トヤマシノブゴケは栽培して殖やしたものは枯れにくい。

コケリウムにとって、トヤマシノブゴケは水陸両用のため非常に使い勝手がよい。また、シート状になったものは崩れにくいため、苔玉などに最適。蓋のある容器、寄せ植えに使ってもよい。

日本全土、台湾、朝鮮に分布する。

They grow as a mat by the side of groves, partly shady slopes in the mountains, and on the surface of rocks. The color changes from yellow-green to dark green, depending on the strength of the sunlight. It can survive even in submerged locations. The stems are 15 cm long, and the leaves are 1 mm long and cover the stems. The common name comes from a kind of fern called Shinobu (*Davallia mariesii*). It is green in wet conditions, but it shrinks immediately in dry conditions. In the winter it turns into a golden color.

If you propagate it at home, it is difficult to keep them from withering. It is very useful to make a moss arrangement, as it can be adapted for amphibious. Also, for Kokedama (moss ball), as the sheet of moss does not brake easily. It is good for plant gathering and requires a container with a lid. It is distributed in all of Japan, Taiwan, and Korea.

コケリウム用　　　　　　　　　　　　　　　　　　　　　　　　　　　　For Moss Terrarium

ネズミノオゴケ　　　　　　　　　　　　　　*Myuroclada maximowiczii*

【鼠の尾苔】

栽培難易度	✿	Difficulty of cultivation
日当り・明るさ	☀☀	Light Intensity
温度	✱	Temperature
湿度	●●	Humidity

Nezuminoogoke

日陰の木の根元、岩の壁面、山道の側溝脇や石垣などにマット状に生える。

日陰では長く垂れ下がり、日が当たる場所では全体の長さが短い。風通しのよい場所を好む。長い個体では4cmほどになる。

全体的に艶のある黒緑色で先のほうは緑色になり、触ると硬い。1mmほどの小さな円形の葉を密に付け、先に行くほど小さくなる。濡れていても乾燥していてもあまり見た目が変わらない。

姿がネズミの尾に似るため和名がネズミノオゴケと付いている。

仮根がつながっているためコケリウムでは使いやすい。蓋のある容器で栽培するとよい。

日本全土、アジア、アラスカに分布。

It grows as a mat on the shade of tree trunks, rock walls, ditch side of mountain roads, and stone walls. It hangs longer in the shade and shorter in the sun light. The longer individual is about 4 cm and it prefers airy places.

Generally, it has glossy, hard, black-green leaves with tinged green on the tip. The tiny 1 mm round shaped leaves densely gather together and it is smaller on the pointed end. It doesn't change color much in wet or dry conditions. The common Japanese name is derived from a mouse-tail. It is easy to use for arrangements as temporary roots are connected. Use containers with a lid. It is distributed all over Japan, Asia, and Alaska.

コケリウム用　　　　　　　　　　　　　　　　　　　　　　For Moss Terrarium

ハイゴケ　　　　　　　　　　　　　　　　　　*Hypnum plumaeforme*

【這苔】

栽培難易度		Difficulty of cultivation
日当り・明るさ		Light Intensity
温度		Temperature
湿度		Humidity

Haigoke

陽当たりのよいなだらかな斜面、アカマツ林にマット状に広がる。

通常黄緑色だが、冬季に紅葉して鮮やかな黄金色になる。乾燥すると縮れ、葉の色が黄色味を増す。茎の長さは10cmほどで、葉は密につく。

自然界ではよく目にする種類だが、ハイゴケは塩素に弱く、水の補給に水道水は使えない。またアルカリ性にも弱く、葉が黄土色になり枯れる。

蒸れに弱いため、コケリウムでは蓋のある容器で栽培するより、岩付けなどの寄せ植えに使うとよい。仮根の水没を嫌うため水が溜まらないようにする。

日本全土のほか、東アジアから東南アジアに分布する。

It covers as a mat on the sunny gentle slopes and red pine woodland. The leaves are usually yellow-green, but it turns into a vivid golden color in the winter. In dry conditions it shrinks and becomes yellowish. On 10cm long stems, the foliage densely attaches.

It can't come in contact with chlorine or alkaline or it will die. It can't tolerate stuffy air, so it is better to make the plant gathering like Iwatsuke (Root over rock: gathering plants on a small rock). It doesn't like to submerge the temporary roots, so be careful not to accumulate the water.

Distributed to all of Japan, and from East Asia to South East Asia.

コケリウム用　　　　　　　　　　　　　　　　　　　　　　　　For Moss Terrarium

コウヤノマンネングサ　　　　　*Climacium japonicum*

【高野之万年草】

栽培難易度	✿ ✿ ✿	Difficulty of cultivation
日当り・明るさ	☀	Light Intensity
温度	✽ ✽	Temperature
湿度	● ●	Humidity

Kouyanomannengusa

　深山の木漏れ日が射す、空気湿度の高い腐葉土に生える。フロウソウの仲間はコケでは珍しく、まるで小さなヤシの木のような姿をしている。

　細い茎が枝分かれし、2.5mmほどの葉を付ける。茎の高さは10cmほど。フジノマンネングサはコウヤノマンネングサより枝分かれが細かく、細い茎の長さは8cmほど。1次体の地下茎は枝分かれして長く伸び、それぞれの先に2次体を地上に伸ばす。2次体の体の寿命は1年〜2年。

　コケリウムでは2次体を成長させ栽培するため、地下茎が伸びる広さが必要。また、コケでは珍しく1次体の地下茎がないと長期栽培ができない。

　北海道から四国に見られ、東アジア、北アメリカに分布する。

It grows on the humus of high humidity in the air with dappled sunlight in the deep mountains. This species of Tree Moss resembles a palm tree. The thin stem branches are 10 cm long with foliage 2.5 mm long. *Pleuroziopsis ruthenica* (Fujinomannengusa) has finer branches than this moss. Stems of P. ruthenica is 8cm long. Primary root systems branch out and elongate. On the tips, the secondary root system emerges above the soil to develop foliage and the lifespan is 1-2 years. Therefore, you need to grow the primary root system for long-term cultivation. Prepare a wide area for the rhizome to grow. It is distributed from Hokkaido to Shikoku, East Asia, and North America.

コケリウム用　　　　　　　　　　　　　　　　　　　　　　　　For Moss Terrarium

ホソバオキナゴケ　　　　　　　　　*Leucobryum juniperoideum*

【細葉翁苔】

栽培難易度　❀ ❀　Difficulty of cultivation
日当り・明るさ ☀　Light Intensity
温度　　　　✱ ✱　Temperature
湿度　　　　●　　Humidity

Hosobaokinagoke

スギの幹の表面や根元、小砂利まじりの土の上に生える。苔庭に多く使われているコケ。スギゴケやスナゴケとともに寺院やコケ庭に使われる3大ゴケの一つ。紅葉したモミジなどの秋の色合いとの取り合わせも美しい。

高さは1〜3cm、葉の長さは4mmほどで針状。葉は、濡れて水分を含むと鮮やかなエメラルドグリーン色、乾燥していると白色に近い半透明なきわめて薄い抹茶色で、乾燥したときの色からオキナゴケ（翁苔）と和名がついている。

コロニーの大きさは通常4cmほど、時にコロニーがつながり合い一面を覆うこともある。

コケリウムでは仮根が水没しない場所に配置するとよい。蒸れに弱い。

日本全土、アジア、ヨーロッパに分布する。

It inhabits on the surface of trunks, root stems of cedar trees, and on the soil mixed with fine gravel. It is often used for moss gardens, and is one of the three main mosses, together with *Polytricum commune* and *Racomitrium japonicum* for temples and moss gardens. It blends well with colored maple trees in autumn. It is 1-3cm high with needle-shaped leaves that are 4 mm long. When it is wet, it is vivid, emerald-green. When it is dry, it becomes nearly whitish, matcha-green. Okinagoke means Old Man's moss in Japanese. The size of the colony is generally 4 cm, but they tend to link together and sometimes cover an entire area. As it hates stuffy air, it is ideal not to submerge the temporary roots. It is distributed in Japan, Asia and Europe.

コケリウム用　　　　　　　　　　　　　　　　　　　　　　　For Moss Terrarium

ホソホウオウゴケ　　　　　　　　　　　　　　　*Fissidens grandifrons*

【細鳳凰苔】

栽培難易度	❋ ❋	Difficulty of cultivation
日当り・明るさ	☀	Light Intensity
温度	✳	Temperature
湿度	💧💧	Humidity

Hosohouougoke

　明るい日陰の水が滲み出る岩盤、滝の側の岩肌、渓流の側の崖に自生する。茎は垂れ下がるように伸び、5cmほどになる。枝分かれはせず、葉は鳥の羽根のように左右に分かれて並び5mmほど。乾燥すると葉の色が黒緑色になる。濡れると光沢のある濃緑色。形が鳥の羽根のように美しい。仲間のホウオウゴケやヒメホウオウゴケは、水のかかる岩肌より少し離れた日陰の粘土質の地面に盛り上がるようにコロニーを作り生える。

　コケリウムでは蓋のある容器で栽培すると良く育つ。仮根が繋がっているため、仮根部をハサミで使う大きさに切る。

　本州から九州に多く分布し、台湾にもある。

It grows by the bedrocks where water oozes out, in semi-shady places, on rocks by waterfalls, and along cliffs near mountain streams. The stems are 5 cm long and they droop down. Each leaf is 5 mm wide and is side by side on the stem. It looks like beautiful bird feathers. The color is black-green when it is dry, and luminous dark-green when it is wet. *Houougoke (F.nobilis)*, or *Himehouougoke (F.gymnogynus)*, rises on a colony in the shady clay soil with dripping water nearby. It grows well in a container with a lid. To cut off the connected temporary roots, you can use a pair of scissors. It grows often from Honshu to Kyusyu, and also in Taiwan.

コケリウム用   For Moss Terrarium

ナガバチヂレゴケ   *Ptychomitrium linearifolium*

栽培難易度	❖ ❖ ❖	Difficulty of cultivation
日当り・明るさ	✦ ✦	Light Intensity
温度	✱ ✱	Temperature
湿度	● ●	Humidity

【長葉縮苔】

Nagabachijiregoke

薄日の射す渓流脇の大きな岩の表面にコロニーが集まり生える。ときに岩を覆うこともある。地面にはほとんど生えない。

乾燥すると葉が縮れてカールし、枯れたように見える。濡れると葉が広がり、まるで岩に生えたマリモのように見える。

茎は4cmほどで枝分かれする。葉は6mmほど針状で下部が膨らむ。

コケリウムではウマスギゴケのように単体ではないため扱いやすい。仮根および葉、茎全体が水没に弱いため、必ず岩の上にや寄せ植えでは水がたま溜まらないようにする。水に浸からなければ、蓋のある容器でも栽培できる。

本州、四国、九州に分布し、朝鮮、中国にもある。

It develops colonies on the surface of large rocks, located in the mountain stream in soft light. Sometimes, it covers all of the rocks. It doesn't grow on the ground. In dry conditions, the foliage shrinks, becomes curly, and looks dead. The foliage spreads out and resembles Aegagropila linnaei, when it's wet. The stem is 4 cm long and branches out. The needle-shaped leaves are 6 mm long and swell on the bottom.

It is easy to handle in a moss terrarium, because it is not an individual plant like Umasugigoke*(P. commune)*. Foliage, stems, and temporary roots have a weakness to submerge, so you need to plant them on the rocks. Be careful not to accumulate the water when you do plant gathering. If it is kept out of water, it can cultivate in a container with a lid. It is distributed in Honshu, Shikoku, Kyusyu, Korea, and China.

アクアリウム・アクアテラリウム用　　　　　　　For Aquarium & Aqua Terrarium

カマサワゴケ　　　　　　　　　　　　　　　*Philonotis falcate*

【鎌沢苔】

栽培難易度	✤ ✤	Difficulty of cultivation
明るさ	☀ ☀	Light Intensity
温度	✱	Temperature
湿度	● ● ●	Humidity

Kamasawagoke

　用水路の水がかかる側溝の壁面、湧き水が流れ出る岩肌に生える。

　赤褐色の茎に、長さ2mmほどの黄緑色のギザギザのある細な葉がたくさんつく。茎の高さは1cm〜5cm。黄緑色の2cm〜5cm前後のコロニーで、群生する。水中に沈水状態でも成長できる。比較的水温が低く、一定の温度を好む。水がつねにかからないと枯れてなくなる。非常に乾燥に弱い。

　アクアテラリウムなどでは、水が高温になると腐り枯れるため、水を循環させ、水槽用のクーラーを設置するとよい。

　日本全土の渓流や水辺、アジア、アフリカに分布する。

It grows on the wall face of a gutter where the water splashes from the irrigation canal, or on a rock face where the spring comes out. It has 2 mm reddish-brown stems that have many fine, yellow-green leaves that have serrated edges. The height is 1-5 cm.
The 2-5 cm yellow-green colonies live in a cluster. It can be grown under the water with a constant water temperature. If the water does not cover it, then it will wither and disappear. If you grow it in an aqua terrarium, then you need to circulate the water and put an aquatic cooler to prevent rotting in high temperatures. It is distributed in all of Japan's mountain stream and waterside, as well as Asia and Africa.

アクアリウム・アクアテラリウム用　　　　For Aquarium & Aqua Terrarium

クロカワゴケ　　　　*Fontinalis antipyretica*

【黒川苔】

栽培難易度		Difficulty of cultivation
明るさ		Light Intensity
温度	✱	Temperature
湿度	●●●	Humidity

Kurokawagoke

　清流の流れ込む小さな小川、湧き水の流れ込む水溜りの小石や砂利にマット状に生える。

　葉の色は黒緑色。茎に3㎜〜8㎜ほどの葉を付ける。茎は長く10㎝ほどになることもある。

　クロカワゴケ、ミズキャラゴケは、アクアリウムショップで販売しているウィローモスの一種で、熱帯魚などをいっしょに飼育し楽しむ水草水槽にもよく使われている。

　アクアリウムなどでに使うとき、在来種は高水温に弱いため、水槽用クーラーを設置して栽培する。水の交換や追加時には、カルキに弱いためカルキ中和剤を入れる。

　北海道、本州、アジア、ヨーロッパ、北アメリカ、アフリカ北部に自生する。

It grows as a mat on the pebbles, gravels by a tiny brook, and clear water from a stream. Foliage is black-green and attaches on the stems that are 3-8 mm long. Sometimes the stems can even become 10 cm long. This and Mizukyaragoke (*Taxiphyllum Barbierii*) are a type of Willow Moss, and they sell it at the aquarium shop. It is often used to keep tropical fish in a water plant aquarium. This Japanese native variety is vulnerable to high water temperature, so you need to use an aquatic cooler. When you change the water, use a chlorine neutralizer. It is distributed in Hokkaido, Honshu, Asia, Europe, North America, and North Africa.

アクアリウム・アクアテラリウム用　　　　　　　For Aquarium & Aqua Terrarium

ホソバミズゼニゴケ

【細葉水銭苔】

Pellia endiviifolia

Hosobamizuzenigoke

栽培難易度　✤✤　Difficulty of cultivation
明るさ　　　☀　Light Intensity
温度　　　　✱　Temperature
湿度　　　💧💧💧　Humidity

　湧き水が流れる側溝、水が染み出る岩場の斜面にへばり付くように生える。通常、10cm前後のコロニーだが、広範囲に広がり生えることもある。

　通常葉の色は明るい緑色だが、紫色を帯びることがあり、別名ムラサキミズゼニゴケとも呼ばれる。葉の長さは2〜5cm、幅7㎜。葉は触ると薄く、意外と脆く崩れやすい。秋から冬にかけて葉状体の先にリボンのような無性芽を付ける。

　アクアテラリウムなどでは葉の形が面白く、水中に浸かっても枯れないため人気がある。なるべく仮根が水に浸かるようにする。高水温には弱い。

　日本全土、中国、インド、ヨーロッパ、北アメリカに分布する。

It clings on the walls of gutters where spring water streams, or where the slopes of rocks ooze-out pure water. Generally, the size of the colony is 10 cm, but it can also spread out in a wide range. Often the foliage is bright green, and sometimes tinged with purple. Murasakimizuzenigoke means purple variety, and this is 2-5cm long with leaves 7 mm wide. It is fragile to touch and easy to crumble. From autumn to winter, it has gemma like a ribbon on top of the thallus. It is popular for making an aqua terrarium, because it can submerge and hold an interesting shape. Try to plant the temporary roots in water. It is weaker in high temperatures. It is distributed in all of Japan, China, India, Europe, and North America.

アクアリウム・アクアテラリウム用　　For Aquarium & Aqua Terrarium

ツルチョウチンゴケ　　*Plagiomnium maximoviczii*

【蔓提灯苔】

栽培難易度	✤ ✤ ✤	Difficulty of cultivation
明るさ	☀	Light Intensity
温度	✱	Temperature
湿度	💧 💧 💧	Humidity

Tsuruchouchingoke

　日陰でつねに濡れた沢の縁の岩、水が滲み出る岩の上に小さなマット状で生える。湧き水や冷たい滲み出した水が溜まる場所にも生える。

　茎は枝分かれし横へと伸び重なる。葉は長さ8mmほどで細長く、透明なエメラルドグリーン色、表面は波打つ。

　アクアテラリウムなどで栽培する場合、高水温に弱いため、水槽用のクーラーを設置するとよい。仮根は水に浸かった状態にするとよい。全体が水中に浸かっても枯れない。乾燥すると葉先から茶色くなり枯れる。枯れた部分はまめにトリミングしないと葉元まで枯れ、全体に広がる。

　日本全土のほか、朝鮮、中国、ロシア、インドに分布する。

It grows on the ridges of rocks in wet conditions with shade, on rocks near rushing water, and in accumulated water. It grows as a small mat shape and has stems that are layered and branch out horizontally. It has 8 mm slender leaves that are transparent, emerald green and rippled on the surface. You need an aquarium cooler to cultivate it in an aqua terrarium, as it is weak to high water temperatures. Plant the temporary roots in water, and the whole plant can be submerged. When it's dry, it withers from the tip of the foliage and turns brown and dies. You need to trim the dead part quickly, because it will spread to the rest of its body. It is distributed in all of Japan, Korea, China, Russia, and India.

アクアリウム・アクアテラリウム用　　　　　For Aquarium & Aqua Terrarium

コツボゴケ　　　　　　　　　　　*Plagiomnium acutum*

【小壺苔】

アクアテラリウムなどで使うときは、水に浸かった状態は避ける。水がかかる場所に配置する。

Kotsubogoke

In an aqua terrarium, do not submerge, but plant it where the water is splashing it.

ネズミノオゴケ　　　　　　　　*Myuroclada maximowiczi*

【鼠の尾苔】

アクアテラリウムなどでは、水面より上に配置する。岩陰など光の当たりにくい場所でも育つ。

Nezuminoogoke

In an aqua terrarium, plant it above the water level. It can be grown on a rock shade with little light.

トヤマシノブゴケ　　　　　　　　*Thuidium kanedae*

【外山忍苔】

アクアテラリウムなどで、水中に浸かった状態でも栽培できる。高水温には弱い。

Toyamashinobugoke

It can grow in submerged conditions, but it is vulnerable to high water temperatures.

ホソホウオウゴケ　　　　　　　*Fissidens grandifrons*

【細鳳凰苔】

アクアテラリウムなどで、水中での栽培が可能。高水温に弱い。

Hosohouougoke

It can be submerged, and it is vulnerable to high water temperatures.

苔庭用　　　　　　　　　　　　　　　　　　　　　　　　For Moss Garden

アラハシラガゴケ　　　　　　　　　　　　*Leucobryum bowringii*

【粗葉白髪苔】

栽培難易度	✤	Difficulty of cultivation
日当り	☀	Light Intensity
温度	✱✱	Temperature
湿度	●	Humidity

Arahashiragagoke

半日陰のスギやカヤの根の際、近くの乾いた土の上にコロニー状に生える。パステルカラーで非常によく目立つ。ホソバオキナゴケよりも太い葉を持ち、葉はゴワゴワした感じで重なり合う。葉は10㎜ほどで針状。高さは1〜2㎝。乾燥した状態では、パステルカラーの薄いミントグリーン色をしている。濡れるとミントグリーン色になる。近い種類にオオシラガゴケがあるが、葉先に小さな突起がたくさんあり表面がザラつく。

コケ庭では独自の色合いが他のコケと異なり、良いアクセントになる。ホソバオキナゴケなどの側に植えるとよい。もともと乾燥した場所に生えるため、庭に使うときは硬質赤玉土や砂を敷いた上に植える。

日本全土、東南アジアに広く分布する。

It grows as a colony in half-shady sites by the trunks of Japanese cedars or Torreya nucifera. Its pastel color stands out and has thicker leaves than Hosobaokinagoke (*L. juniperoideum*). It has a rough texture and the foliage is layered. The 10 mm long needle shaped leaves are 1-2 cm high. When it is dry, it has a pale, mint-green color. But when it is wet, it has a strong mint-green color. Ooshiragagoke (*L. scabrum*) is a near variety, but it has tiny projections on the tip which make it rough on the surface. Its distinctive color adds good accents in moss gardens. It matches very well with Hosobaokinagoke (*L. juniperoideum*). Since it inhabits in dry places, it may be better to cover with red clay soil or sand, and plant on top of it. It is distributed in all of Japan and South East Asia.

苔庭用　　　　　　　　　　　　　　　　　　　　　　　　　　　　For Moss Garden

カモジゴケ　　　　　　　　　*Dicranum scoparium*

【髭苔】

栽培難易度	✤✤	Difficulty of cultivation
日当り	☀	Light Intensity
温度	✱	Temperature
湿度	●●	Humidity

Kamojigoke

アカマツ林やカラマツ林、亜高山帯または深山の木の根元や、落ち葉の堆積した上にコロニーで生える。シッポゴケやオオシッポゴケといっしょに混生している場所もある。日陰を好む。

茎の高さは8cmほどで、葉の長さは8mmほど、細く尖る。色は濁った緑色。シッポゴケなどと違い、葉先が同じ方向に向くので区別ができる。乾燥していると、葉を巻き上げる。コケ庭では硬質赤玉土小粒を敷き、コロニーごと乗せて軽く手の平で押さえて馴染ませる。仮根がなるべく用土に埋まるようにする。直射日光が当たらないように周りに山野草を植えるとよい。

日本全土、ニュージーランド、北半球に広く分布。

You can find it as colonies in a red pinewood, larch forest, subalpine belt, and by the trunks of trees in the deep mountainside and in accumulated dead leaves. It is often mixed with Shippogoke *(D. japonicum)* and Ooshippogoke *(D.nipponense)*, and it prefers shade. It has stems 8 cm high and leaves 8 mm long, which are thin, pointed, and a cloudy green color. You can identify it by it's foliage that faces the same direction. When it's dry, the leaves become curly. In a moss garden, lay out red clay soil and plant as a colony. Push gently with palms to make fit in, and surround it with wild flowers to prevent the direct sunlight. It is distributed in all of Japan, New Zealand and the Northern Hemisphere.

苔庭用　　　　　　　　　　　　　　　　　　　　　　　　　For Moss Garden

シッポゴケ

Dicranum japonicum

【尻尾苔】

Shippogoke

栽培難易度	✿ ✿	Difficulty of cultivation
日当り	☀	Light Intensity
温度	✳	Temperature
湿度	● ●	Humidity

日差しの射さない明るい、ときどき霧の発生する湿った腐葉土の上に、群落を作る。亜高山帯に比較的多い。

茎は直立し10cmほどになる。茎の表面に白い仮根があるため、似ている種類と区別しやすい。

葉は細長く、長さは10mmほど。葉の色は鮮やかな緑色。

コケ庭では硬質赤玉土小粒を敷き、なるべくコロニーを崩さないまま用土に乗せ、軽く手の平で押さえて馴染ませる。仮根がなるべく用土に埋まるようにする。明るい日陰が適してる。つねに湿った状態は嫌うため、乾いたらたっぷり水を与える。高温多湿に弱く、蒸れると茶色になり枯れる。傷むと広がりやすいため、早めにに取り除く。

北海道から九州、朝鮮、中国に分布する。

It creates plant communities on moist humus, where there is no direct sun. It occurs comparatively on a subalpine belt. The Upright stems elongate 10 cm, and they have white temporary roots, which is similar to other plants. The 10 mm leaves are slender and have a vivid green color. In moss gardens, lay out red clay soil and gently place on top trying not to break the colony. Gently push with your palms making sure the temporary roots are buried in the soil. It is ideal in semi-shade, and when it's dry you need to soak them thoroughly with water. It does not resist of high temperature and humidity, and stuffy plants turn brown and wither. Since the damage tends to spread, remove affected area as soon as possible. It is distributed from Hokkaido to Kyushu, Korea, and China.

苔庭用　　　　　　　　　　　　　　　　　　　　　　　　　　　　For Moss Garden

タマゴケ

Bartramia pomiformis

【玉苔】

日陰の風通しのよいところに配置する。高温多湿を嫌う。

栽培難易度	✤✤	Difficulty of cultivation
日当り	☀	Light Intensity
温度	✳	Temperature
湿度	●	Humidity

Tamagoke

It does not like high temperatures and high humidity, so keep it in shady and airy places.

ホソバオキナゴケ

Leucobryum juniperoideum

【細葉翁苔】

日陰の風通しのよいところに配置する。つねに濡れた状態は嫌う。

栽培難易度	✤	Difficulty of cultivation
日当り	☀	Light Intensity
温度	✳✳	Temperature
湿度	●	Humidity

Hosobaokinagoke

It doesn't like to be consistently wet, so keep it in airy and shady places.

ハイゴケ

Hypnum plumaeforme

【這苔】

明るい湿ったところに配置する。蒸れに弱い。見た目は良くないが、少し乾かし気味がよい。

栽培難易度	✤✤	Difficulty of cultivation
日当り	☀☀	Light Intensity
温度	✳✳	Temperature
湿度	●●	Humidity

Haigoke

Keep it in light and moist places, but it is weak in humidity. Although it doesn't look nice, it is also good to keep it semi-dry conditions.

エゾスナゴケ

Racomitrium japonicum

【蝦夷砂苔】

日当たりがよく、風通しのよいところに配置する。乾いた状態を好む。ときどきたっぷりと水を与える。

栽培難易度	✤✤	Difficulty of cultivation
日当り	☀☀☀	Light Intensity
温度	✳✳	Temperature
湿度	●	Humidity

Ezosunagoke

Keep it in sunny, airy, and dry conditions. Give them plenty of water from time to time.

苔庭用　　　　　　　　　　　　　　　　　　　　　　　　For Moss Garden

ウマスギゴケ　　　　　　　　　　　　　*Polytrichum commune*

【馬杉苔】

湿度の高い、明るい場所に配置する。ハイゴケといっしょに植えると、やがて枯れてなくなる。

Umasugigoke

It grows well with high humidity and bright light. If you plant it with Haigoke (*Hypnum plumaeforme*), it will eventually die.

コツボゴケ　　　　　　　　　　　　　　*Plagiomnium acutum*

【小壺苔】

日陰の湿った場所に配置する。乾燥に非常に弱いため、まめに水を与える。

Kotsubogoke

Put it in a shady and moist place. It is very weak to dryness, so you need to water it often.

トヤマシノブゴケ　　　　　　　　　　　*Thuidium kanedae*

【外山忍苔】

湿った日陰に配置するとよい。明るい場所では枯れないが、葉が黄色くなる。

Toyamashinobugoke

Put it in a moist and shady place. Though it doesn't die in light places, the foliage turns yellow.

ヒノキゴケ　　　　　　　　　　　　　　*Trachycystis microphylla*

【檜苔】

明るい風通しのよい場所に配置する。あまりジメジメしていると枯れる。

Hinokigoke

Keep it in light and airy places, because it will wither in damp conditions.

ヨーロッパの苔図鑑　　　　　　　　　　　　　　　　　Guide Book of European Moss

バンクヘアキャップ　　　　　　　*Polytrichastrum formosum*

落ち葉の積もった林に多く生える。
日本のオオスギゴケに近い種類。
鮮やかな針状の葉を放射状に付ける。

Bank Haircap It grows in the forest on accumulated dead leaves. The vivid needle-like leaves develop radially on the stems. It is near to Oosugigoke (*P. formosum Hedw*) in Japan.

ビッグシャギーモス　　　　　　　*Rhytidiadelphus triquetrus*

ライムストーン（石灰岩）の上に生える。
日本のオオフサゴケに近い種類。
茎が赤いのが特徴的。

Big shaggy moss It inhabits on limestone and it is near to Oofusagoke (*R. triquetrus*) in Japan. Red stems are a distinctive character of the moss.

ヨーロッパの苔図鑑　　　　　　　　　　　　　Guide Book of European Moss

スワンズネックタイムモス　　　　　　　*Mnium hornum*

ライムストーンの上や石垣に、　　　**Swan's-neck Thyme-moss** It inhabits to
小さなコロニーを作って生える。　　create little colonies on limestone and stonewalls. Near variety
日本のオオヤマチョウチンゴケに近い種類。of Japan is called Ooyamatyotingoke (*M.hornum*)

ラフストークトゥフェザーモス　　　　　*Brachythecium rutabulum*

枯れ枝にツリー状に付く。　　　　　**Rough-Stalked Feather-moss** It hangs on
日本のヒロハノフサゴケと近い種類。　dead trees, and its yellowish foliage is literally like a feather. It is
葉は黄色味がかり羽状に付く。　　　similar to Japanese Hirohanohusagoke (*B. rutabulum*).

ヨーロッパの苔図鑑　　　　　　　　　　　Guide Book of European Moss

ブライム モス　　　　　　　　　　　***Bryum capillare***

石垣や岩の表面にに生える。
日本のハリガネゴケに近い種類。

Bryum Moss It inhabits on the surface of stone walls and rocks. Which is near variety of Japanese Hariganegoke(*Bryum capillare*).

アップルモス　　　　　　　　　　　***Bartramia pomiformis***

林の縁や木の根元に、コロニーを作り点在する。
日本のタマゴケに近い種類。

Apple Moss It is scattered near the edges of woodland and base of trees. It is similar to Tamagoke (*Bartamia pomiformis*.) in Japan.

ヨーロッパの苔図鑑　　　　　　　　　　Guide Book of European Moss

クリーピングフィンガーワート　　*Lepidozia reptans*

ムチゴケ科の日本のハイスギゴケに近い種類。イギリスの気候の違いのためか、日本の同種よりやや小型で、あまり茎を伸ばさない。

Creeping Fingerwart It is similar to Haisugigoke *(L. reptans)* of *Lapidoziacea* in Japan. When you compare to the Japanese relative, it is smaller and has shorter stems because of the climate difference.

オルトトリクム レイリア　　*Ortotrikhum layelya*

石垣の上に広がり生える。非常に生え方に特徴がある。日本のタチヒダゴケの仲間。

Ortotrikhumm layelya It spreads out on stonewalls and it is very distinctive in the growing process. It is a variety of Tatihidagoke *(O.consobrinum)* in Japan.

77

ヨーロッパの苔図鑑　　　　　　　　　　　　　　Guide Book of European Moss

フラジル ケンフィロプス モス　　　　　*Campylopus fragilis*

石垣の隙間や上に、コロニー状に生える。日本のマユハケゴケに近い種類。

Fragile Campylopus Moss It inhabits in the gap of the stonewalls or on the wall itself. It is similar to Mayuhakegoke *(Campylopus fragilis)* in Japan.

コモンタマリスクモス　　　　　　　　　　　*Thuidium tamariscinum*

林の縁に多く生える。日本のオオシノブゴケに近い種類。ミストや霧が多いため、日本の同種より大きい。

Common Tamarisk-moss It commonly grows on the edge of woodlands, and is similar to Ooshinobugoke *(T.tamariscinum)* in Japan. British variety is greater, as mist and fog occurs more often in the UK.

ヨーロッパの苔図鑑　　　　　　　　　　　　　　Guide Book of European Moss

コモンフェザーモス　　　　　　*Kindbergia praelonga*

大きな群落となり、林の淵に大きな群落を作り広がる。日本のナガナギゴケに近い種類。

Common Feather-moss It becomes a huge cluster and inhabits by deep bodies of water in the woodlands. It is similar to Naganagigoke (*K.praelonga*)in Japan.

スプレンディド フェザー モス　　　*Hylocomium splendens*

小さな木のような姿のコケ。林に地面を覆うように纏まって生える。日本のイワダレゴケに近い種類。

Splendid Feather-Moss It is like a tiny tree, and it covers the ground of the forest. Near variety of Japan is Iwadaregoke (*H.splendens*).

79

ヨーロッパの苔図鑑　　　　　Guide Book of European Moss

オーバーリーフペリア　　　　*Pellia epiphylla*

沢にあ近る石を覆うように生える。
日本に自生する縁種はホソバミズゼニゴケ。
イギリスの種類はミズゼニゴケ。

Overleaf Pellia　It covers stones and looks like the moss is crawling in a swamp. It is similar to the Endive Pellia (*P.endiviifolia*) of Japan.

ウェイブドシルクモス　　　　*Plagiothecium undulatum*

根元に近い幹に多く生える。
日本のミヤマサナダゴケに近い種類。
枝先の葉は緑色から白色に変わる。

Waved Silk-moss　It inhabits near the foot of trees, and the tips of the leaves change from green to white. It is similar to Miyamasanadagoke (*P.nemorale*) in Japan.

ヨーロッパの苔図鑑　　　　　　　　　Guide Book of European Moss

コモンスムースキャップ　　　*Atrichum undulatum*

木の根元の周りや、倒木との間に生える。
日本のナミガタタチゴケに近い種類。

Common Smoothcap It inhabits around the foot of trees or between fallen trees. It is similar to Namigatatatigoke *(A.undulatum)* in Japan.

コンプレスドゥエントドンモス　　　*Entodon challengeri*

木の表面や切り株に広がり生える。
日本のヒロハツヤゴケに近い種類。

Compressed entodon moss It spreads over the surface and foot of trees. It is similar to Hirohatuyagoke *(Entodon challenger)* of Japan.

81

パルダリウム

　ビバリウムにはアクアリウム・アクアテラリウム・テラリウムがあります。また、蓋をしないオープンアクアリウム・オープンアクアテラリウム・オープンテラリウムなどもあります。
　そのなかの、テラリウムは19世紀イギリスのロンドンでナサニエル・バグショー・ウォード外科医によって発明されました。
　テラリウムにおいて主体が植物の場合をパルダリウムといいます。
　パルダリウムではラン類やコケ類、高山植物等の自生地を再現し栽培します。この場合クーラーやヒーター、霧発生装置等を使い自生地の温度や湿度までも同じ環境を作ります。そのため、暑さや寒さに弱い植物も栽培できます。基本的には蓋をするため水槽内の湿度がほぼ一定になりラン類やコケ類の栽培に適しているのです。
　あくまでもビバリウムは自然界の環境を再現し、栽培または飼育するシステムの一つです。
　ビバリウムはガラスやアクリルで作られた水槽内に土や砂を入れますが、外にこぼれないので、玄関やリビングなどに小さな癒しの空間を作ることができます。そのため自然や安らぎを求める人たちに人気が出ています。

Paludarium

Vivariums are glass cases used to display or breed plants. There are three types of vivarium: Aquariums, Aqua terrariums and Terrariums. There are also Open aquariums, Open aqua terrariums, and Open terrariums. Terrarium (Wardian case) was invented by Dr. Nathaniel Bagshow Ward (1791-1868) in London.
If the growing species are mainly plants, it is called Paludarium, which is the way to display the habitat of orchids, mosses, and alpine plants. In this case, it is necessary to create the same condition as their vegetation. Therefore, you need to install an air conditioner, heater, or spraying device to grow the plants that cannot survive in cold or hot weather. Basically, if you put the lid on the tank, humidity becomes constant and cultivates orchids or mosses. Vivalium is a way to grow plants or to rear creatures in a reproduced native environment. As you put soil or sand in a case of an acrylic sheet glass, you don't need to worry about it getting dirty. You can create a tiny peaceful paradise of your own. It is very popular with those who enjoy the nature and seek after tranquility.

コケリウムアレンジ

コケリウム

アクアリウム

苔庭

Beautiful Collection of Moss Terrariums

Weissia cirrata 1805年 ジェームズ・サワビー

コケリウムアレンジ
つくる机

　この机は雪割草研究実験ハウス内にあります。

　ふだん、コケリウムの製作やコケの実験、雪割草（Hepatica）の品種改良、交配やラベル書き、植物研究をする私の机です。

　机の周りには必要な世界地図、黒板、秘境で探し当てた水晶や鉱石、中にはサンカラストーンなども置いています。また、明治時代の高山植物図鑑など、昔の書物も研究には必要なため置いています。もちろん、コケリウムを作るために生育実験している試験管や薬瓶もたくさんあります。

　コケリウムを作るうえで必ず心がけていることがあります。

　それは、コケリウムは生け花ではなく、コケ植物の生育を楽しむ栽培の一つであるということです。私のコケリウムを手にした方や生徒さんが1年、2年経っても綺麗な状態の作品を楽しめるように心がけ、この机で長く栽培できる方法を考えています。アクアリウムの技術や山野草栽培、盆栽栽培、料理の技術を取り入れた複合的なコケリウムの作り方を開発し、皆さまに楽しんでいただけたらと思っています。

My Desk For Arranging Moss Terrariums

This is located in the Green House of my Hepatica Researching Laboratory. Usually, I work here for creating moss terrariums, breeding Hepaticas, and researching general plants. My desk is surrounded by a world map, a black board, and some crystals and precious minerals I discovered in secluded regions. I collected alpine plants and picture books of oldies for my researching. You can also find test tubes or medicine bottles for making terrariums. One thing I always keep in my mind is I am not making flower arrangements, but instead observing and enjoying the process of breeding mosses.
I always try to find the best way to keep my living art of moss terrariums, which usually last for a few years. This is the place of my inspiration and experimentation.
I made efforts to design the best growing method for moss terrariums through my knowledge of wild flower growing methods, Bonsai gardening, and even cooking.

arrange 1　ファンとモスⅠ
arrange 2　ファンとモスⅡ
arrange 3　ファンとモスⅢ

Design1　Fern and Moss Ⅰ
Design2　Fern and Moss Ⅱ
Design3　Fern and Moss Ⅲ

形の違う小さなガラスの器に、ネズミノオゴケとケヘチマゴケを使い、トキワシノブといっしょに寄せ植えしました。
　グレーの石を入れることで自然な感じになります。ちょっと、玄関やリビングの窓辺にあるだけで癒されます。

In the glassware of different shapes, I displayed *Myuroclada maximowiczii*, *Pohlia flexuosa*, and *Davallia tyermanii*.
The grey stone gives off a natural feeling, and it can be your own peaceful corner at home.

86

arrange 1
ケヘチマゴケ、トキワシノブ

Design1 Tokiwashinobu (*Humata tyermannii*) and Kehechimagoke (*Pohlia flexuosa*)

arrange 2
ケヘチマゴケ、
トキワシノブ

Design2
Tokiwashinobu
(*Humata tyermannii*) and
Kehechimagoke
(*Pohlia flexuosa*)

arrange 3
ネズミノオゴケ、
トキワシノブ

Design3
Tokiwashinobu
(*Humata tyermannii*) and
Nezuminoogoke
(*Myuroclada maximowiczii*)

87

arrange 4　トリオ オブ ラカンマキ　　　　　　　　　　Design4 Trio of Rakanmaki (*Podocarpus macrophyllus*)

arrange 4
ラカンマキ、ケヘチマゴケ

Design4
Rakanmaki (*Pohlia flexuosa*)
Hechimagoke (*Pohlia flexuosai*)

　ガラスの可愛いキャンドル立てに、ラカンマキの実生苗をケヘチマゴケといっしょに植えました。
　コケリウム用に、樹木のタネを蒔いておくと、作品作りに使えます。
　落葉樹では紅葉が素敵なモミジやサクラ、コナラ、バラなど。常緑樹なら、ナギやモチノキ、針葉樹なら、アカマツやサワラ、モミなどがお勧めです。また、ツツジの仲間のミヤマキリシマ、アジサイの仲間のヤマアジサイは挿し木をして小さな苗を作ることをお勧めします。

I planted a seedling of *Podocarpus macrophyllus* together with *Pohlia flexuosa*, in a lovely glass candle stand. It is useful to use the seeds from the trees for making moss terrarium. Maple trees, Cherry trees, *Quercuss serrata*, and Roses are good choices of deciduous trees. I also recommend conifers like Red pine, Sawara cypress, and Fir. If you like to have *Rododendron kiusaianum* or *Hydrangea serrata*, take a cutting to prepare small sized plants.

arrange 5　ボタニカル モス ドーム　　　　　Design5 Botanical Moss Dome ~ Glass Dome with Base

arrange 5
ナガバチヂレゴケ

Design5
Nagabachijiregoke (*Ptychomitrium linearifolium*)

　高さのあるガラスドームに、コケの生えた岩山を作りました。
　ナガバチヂレゴケは、湿度が高いと葉を開き綺麗な姿になります。
　ガラスドームは湿度を保つのに好適です。保水性のある溶岩を使うことで、水を与える頻度が軽減されます。
　溶岩は産地によっては非常に酸性度が高いものがあるため気をつけましょう。
　詳しい作り方は P126 に、わかりやすく紹介しています。
　高さ約 250㎜

This looks like a tiny version of a rocky mountain covered with moss in a dome of 250 mm high. *Ptychomitrium linearifolium* opens beautiful leaves in humid places, and a glass dome is ideal to keep constant humidity.
If you use rocks with water retention, you can reduce frequency of watering. But be careful because lava rocks are sometimes too acidic.
No.4 The Rocky Mountain style Moss Terrarium in a glass dome is referenced on P126. See this page for more details.

89

arrange 6　アンブレラ ワールド　　　　　　　　　　　　　　Desin6. Umbrella World

arrange 6
オオカサゴケ

Design6
Ookasagoke (*Rhodobryum giganteum.*)

　木製の蓋のあるガラスのポプリ入れに、オオカサゴケの森を作りました。オオカサゴケは魅力的な形です。あえて、このオオカサゴケだけをたくさん使ったコケリウムはなんとも贅沢な逸品です。
　湿度が保たれていると、光沢のある葉をピンと開いて綺麗です。1種類だけを入れて楽しむコケリウムは自生地そのもののようになり、陳列するとまるで博物館のようです。
　詳しい作り方はP130に、わかりやすく紹介しています。
　＊撮影のため、蓋を外してます。
　高さ約 200㎜

This glassware has a wooden lid and is 200 mm high. I created the wood of *Rhodobryum giganteum*, and it is gorgeous to use only this one . If the moist is constant, it keeps the glossy foliage pulled tight. It looks lovely and almost looks like a museum that recreates a native scenery.
No.6 *Rhodobryum giganteum* and Striped Pattern Stone Moss (P130) is easy to understand how to make it.
　*I removed the lid for photography.

arrange 7 アメジスト マウンテン　　　　　　　　　　Design7. Amethyst Mountain

arrange 7
ケヘチマゴケ

Design7
Kehechimagoke (*Pohlia flexuosa*)

　取っ手が綺麗なガラスのポプリ入れにコケリウムを作りました。
　長い年月の間に海の波で研磨され、結晶が丸くなった紫水晶を中心に配置しました。周りには緑が美しいケヘチマゴケを用いアレンジしました。コケリウムの中に鉱石や宝石の原石などを入れても素敵なアレンジになります。
　詳しい作り方はP128に、わかりやすく紹介しています。
　高さ約140㎜

Used the pretty glassware of pot-pourri that is 140 mm high. I designed it by placing the round Amethyst crystal in the center, and then surrounded it with *Pohlia flexuosa*, which is a beautiful green color. It is a good idea to put your favorite minerals or precious stones inside to make it more interesting.
Detail of how to make is on No.5 Purple Moss Crystal Terrarium (P128)

arrange 8　モス ウェイブ ラグーン　　　　　　Design8. Moss Wave Lagoon

　　レトロ風な金魚鉢に、涼しげな海辺をイメージしてアレンジしました。オオカサゴケはヤシの木のイメージ、ホソホウオウゴケは岩に押し寄せる波しぶきのイメージで。
　　金魚鉢のように上部が一度すぼまった器は、湿度を保ちやすいので、湿気が好きな種類のコケにはちょうど良いです。ネコの置物を縁に付けると、さあ、ものがたりの始まりです。

Inside a nostalgic gold fish glassware, I designed an image of a lagoon with a cool sea breeze. *Rhodobryum giganteum* is the image of a palm tree. *Fissidens grandifrons* is the image of waves on the seashore. This kind of container with a narrow mouth on top keeps moist easier and is ideal for the moss that likes humidity. A story will begin once you put a cat figure on the terrarium!

arrange 8
オオカサゴケ、ホソホウオウゴケ

Design8
Ookasagoke (*Rhodobryum giganteum*)
Hosohouougoke (*Fissidens grandifrons*)

arrange 9 ザ モス アイランド 　　　　　　　　Design9. The Moss Island

arrange 9
オオカサゴケ、コツボゴケ

Design9
Ookasagoke (*Rhodobryum giganteum*)
Kouyanomannengusa(*Cimacium japaonicum*)

　夏をイメージしての作品には、オオカサゴケやコウヤノマンネングサなど、樹木のような形のコケが似合います。
　乾燥するとチリチリになり見た目が悪いため、アレンジする時はなるべく湿度が保てる、湿気が逃げにくい形状の器を使うとよいです。また、アレンジしたコケの周りに水が溜まると乾燥を防げます。そんな意味でも、このキャンドルグラスは最適です。
　詳しい作り方は P122 に、わかりやすく紹介しています。

If you want to make a tropical feeling of summer, you can use the tree like moss as *Rhodobryum giganteum* or *Cimacium japaonicum*. You need to use a container to make constant humidity. In dry conditions, the mosses look curly and become ugly. If the water is accumulated around them, you can keep it moist. Therefore, the candle containers are ideal for it.
Reference is No, 2 Water-loving Moss Terrarium (P122)

arrange10 コケと砂浜Ⅰ
arrange11 コケと砂浜Ⅱ

Design10 Moss and Sandy beach Ⅰ
Design11 Moss and Sandy beach Ⅱ

arrange10
左上 ヒノキゴケ
arrange11
右下 シッポゴケ、ホソホウオウゴケ

Design10
　Upper Left Hinokigoke (*Pyrrhobryum dozyaum*)
Design11
　Bottom Right Sippogoke (*Dicranum japonicum*)
　　　　　　Hosohouougoke (*Fissidens grandifrons*)

　上部がすぼまったガラスの器2つに、種類の異なるコケをアレンジしました。白い微小な寒水石を敷き砂浜をイメージしました。
　ヒノキゴケやシッポゴケは仮根部が傷むと枯れやすいため、ゼオライトを器の底と周りに入れてあります。葉先が巻いてきたら、葉全体に霧吹きで水を与えます。あまりに乾燥するときは透明なアクリル板やガラス板で蓋をするとよいです。ガラス板などがないときは、ラップでも大丈夫です。

I have designed two types of moss in the mouth squeezed glassware. Lay out tiny white stones (Kansuiseki) to look like a sandy beach. I put zeolite on the bottom and around the container for protecting temporary roots of *Pyrrhobryum dozyaum* and *Dicranum japonicum*. They are fragile and easily withered.
When they become curly, spray the mist. If it is too dry, you can put a lid on it with an acrylic or glass board. You can also use the cling film.

arrange 12　コケとシダの囁きⅠ	Design12 Whisper of Moss and Fern Ⅰ
arrange 13　コケとシダの囁きⅡ	Design13 Whisper of Moss and Fern Ⅱ
arrange 14　コケとシダの囁きⅢ	Design14 Whisper of Moss and Fern Ⅲ

arrange12
　左　コウヤノマンネングサ、カタヒバ
arrange13
　中央　シッポゴケ、モウコヒトツバ
arrange14
　右　ウマスギゴケ、コンテリクラマゴケ

Design 12
　Left　Kouyanomannengusa (*Cimacium japonicum*)
　　　　Katahiba (*Selaginella moellendorffii*)
Design 13
　Middle　Sippogoke (*Dicranum japonicum*)
　　　　　Moukohitotuba (*Pyrrosia petiolosa*)
Design 14
　Right　Umasugigoke (*Polytrichum commune*)
　　　　　Konterikuramagoke (*Selaginella uncinata*)

　パステルカラーでペイントされたモルタルの器に、種類の異なるコケとシダを寄せ植えしました。
　1つ目は樹木のような形のコウヤノマンネングサとレースのようなカタヒバ、
　2つ目は動物のシッポに似たシッポゴケと海藻のコブのような形のモウコヒトツバ、
　3つ目はスギの苗木に似たウマスギゴケと青味のある葉の色が魅力的なコンテリクラマゴケです。形の異なるコケやシダを組み合わせてアレンジするのも楽しいです。

In the mortared containers, I planted gatherings of several mosses and ferns. First one is a tree-shaped *Cimacium japonicum* and lace-like *Selaginella moellendorffii*. The second one is a plant gathering like an animal's tail *Dicranum japaonicum* and seaweed hump like *Pyrrosia petiolosa*. The third one is the gathering of cider seedling like *Polytrichum commune* and *Selaginella uncinata*, which has an attractive, bluish foliage. It is quite fun to arrange these different species all together.

arrange15　苔森の魅惑の苺　　　　　　　　　　　Design 15 Charming Strawberries in the Mossy Forest

錆びたブリキ缶の底に穴を開けて、花が咲く前に、ノウゴウイチゴとトヤマシノブゴケを植えました。

たくさんの真っ赤なイチゴが実り、緑色のコケに映えます。イチゴはいろいろな生き物のご馳走です。果実がある時期は、室内の窓辺に置き楽しみましょう。

山野草と寄せ植えする時は、なるべく、花が咲く前までにアレンジします。また種類によっては、根をいじられるのが嫌いな植物もあります。

I made a hole on the bottom of a rusted tin can, and planted *Fragaria iinumae* and *Thuidium kanedae*. I harvested plenty of strawberries and it so vivid with the green moss. It may attract birds or other animals, if you put it by the windowsill with berries inside. You can create this before you add the flowers. Be careful for handling, because some plants and roots may not like to be messed with.

arrange15
トヤマシノブゴケ、ノウゴウイチゴ

Design15
Toyamashinobugoke (*Thuidium kanedae*)
Hinokigoke (*Pyrrhobryum dozyanum*) , Nougouichigo (*Fragaria iinumae*)

arrange16　苔森の黒い果実

Design 16. Blackberry in the Mossy Forest

陶器でできたバスケット風の植木鉢に、ブラックベリーとトヤマシノブゴケ、ヒノキゴケをアレンジしました。

ブラックベリーは北アメリカやヨーロッパの森に多く自生します。

収穫した果実は、砂糖と少量のレモン汁で煮詰めジャムにします。イギリスではアフタヌーンティータイムで、スコーンにクロテッドクリームといっしょに乗せて食べると、酸味と香りが絶妙です。

In a basket-like flowerpot, I arranged blackberries, *Thuidium kanedae* and *Pyrrhobryum dozyanum*. Blackberry is common in the woodland of Europe, and it can be made delicious jam. I like its fragrance and sour taste on top of scones with clotted cream.

arrange16
トヤマシノブゴケ、ヒノキゴケ、ブラックベリー

Design16
Toyamashinobugoke (*Thuidium kanedae*), Hinokigoke (*Pyrrhobryum dozyanum*) and Blackberry.

arrange17 風そよぐ小さな湿地　　　　　　　　　　　　　Design 17 Breezy Little Wetland

arrange17
トヤマシノブゴケ、ヒメワタスゲ

Design17
Toyamashinobugoke (*Thuidium kanedae.*)
Himewatasuge (*Trichophorum alpinum*)

　清々しい高原の湿地帯をイメージして、浅い山草鉢にヒメワタスゲとトヤマシノブゴケを植えました。
　ヒメワタスゲはホタルイ属の植物です。尾瀬などで観察できるワタスゲはワタスゲ属なため少し違います。
　7月頃に開花した穂から、白い糸を出し綿菓子のように見えます。
　半日陰で栽培し、植えるときに少し大きめの石を入れ頭を出しておきます。日中、熱を逃がす役目をします。夕方、たっぷり水を与えます。

I designed it from the image of a refreshing wetland in a highland. I planted *Trichophorum alpinum* together with *Thuidium kanedae*. *Eriophorum vaginatum* can be seen in Oze highland in Japan, which is different from T. alpinum. It lowers in July and it looks like cotton candies. When you plant this, put a big stone near it and pop its head out, to help release the heat. Grow it in a partly-shady place and water thoroughly in the evening.

98

arrange18 白い三本ブラシ　　　　　　　　　　　　　　Design 18. Three White Blushes

arrange18
ホソバオキナゴケ、コシキジマシライトソウ

Design18
Hosobaokinagoke (*Leucobryum juniperoideum*)
Koshikijimashiraitoso (*Chionographis japonica*)

　釉薬のかかった小品盆栽鉢に、コシキジマシライトソウとホソバオキナゴケを植えました。
　白くブラシのような花弁が特徴のシライトソウ。そのシライトソウのなかで、コシキジマシライトソウは鹿児島県の甑島にしか生えない珍しいシライトソウです。
　非常に背が小さく可愛いです。また、開花期も少し遅いです。
　小さな鉢にアレンジした作品は、水枯れしやすいので、普通サイズの鉢よりこまめに乾き具合をチェックして、乾いていたら、たっぷり水を与えます。

On a tiny glazed Bonsai pot, I planted *Chionographis japonica* and *Leucobryum juniperoideum*. White, blush-like flowers are very distinct and create a variety that you can't find anywhere else, except Koshiki Island. It is tiny and lovely, and blooms with flowers later. If you put mosses in a tiny pot, they dehydrate sooner than in a larger pot. You need to check it frequently and water thoroughly, if it is dry.

arrange19　月光(風そよぐ夜に)　　　　　　　　　Design 19 On a Breezy Moonlit Night

葉や草姿がササに似ているイネ科のチゴザサを、トヤマシノブゴケで包み苔玉にしました。
スチール製の小物立てを受け皿にして、少し和風とは違う雰囲気に。チゴザサは枝が細いので少しの風でもユラユラします。
お月見しながら、風にそよぐ姿を楽しんでみてはいかがでしょうか。
詳しい作り方はP120に、わかりやすく紹介しています。

I made a moss ball with *Isachne globose*, resembling bamboo leaves and *Thuidium kanedae*. I used the steel plate to make it a bit different from the typical Japanese feeling. A little breeze can wave the thin stems of I. globose, so why don't you enjoy it while you are watching the moon? Reference No. 1 - It is easy to make Moss Balls (P120)

arrange19
トヤマシノブゴケ、チゴザサ

Design19
Toyamashinobugoke (*Thuidum kanedae*)
Chigozasa (*Isachne globose*)

arrange20　コケの小鉢Ⅰ
arrange21　コケの小鉢Ⅱ

Design 20 Moss in a small pot Ⅰ
Design 21 Moss in a small pot Ⅱ

白い小鉢に、小さなコケの丘を作りました。

1つの小鉢にはウマスギゴケを、もう1つの小鉢にはヒノキゴケとナミガタタチゴケを植えました。コケの周りには小石を敷き用土が溢れるのを防ぎます。

陶器はガラスのように透明でないため、中の湿り具合が分かりません。水の与え過ぎで仮根が傷まないように、小鉢の底にはゼオライトを入れます。

In a tiny white pot, I created a little hill. In the first one, I put *Polytrichum commune*, and in the other one I planted *Pyrrhobyyum dozyanum* and *Atrichum undulatum*. I placed pebbles around the mosses to prevent the soil from overflowing. Pottery is not as transparent as glassware, so you won't be able to see the moist conditions. Put zeolite to prevent the temporary roots from being damaged.

arrange20
ウマスギゴケ

Design 20
Umasugigoke
(*Polytrichum commune*)

arrange21
ヒノキゴケ
ナミガタタチゴケ

Design 21
Hinokigoke
(*Pyrrhobryum dozyanum*)
Namigatatachigoke
(*Atrichum undulatum*)

101

arrange 22　センペルビュームにコケを添えて
arrange 23　サボテンときどきコケ？
arrange 24　コケと多肉のキャッスル

Design 22.　Add Moss to Sempervivum
Design 23.　Cacti sometimes Moss?
Design 24.　Castle of Cacti and Succulents

　　多肉植物やサボテンと、コケとは滅多に寄せ植えにはしません。それは栽培環境があまりに違うからです。
　もし、いっしょに栽培できたら、今まで見たことのない新しいコケリウムになります。
　試行錯誤しなができた作品です。
　詳しい作り方はP140に、わかりやすく紹介しています。

Do not plant succulents, Cacti, and Mosses together, or at least don't do it very often, because the cultivation environment is vastly different.
If you can grow them together, it could be a rare new scenery. I tried to do my best with trial and error, so here is my art.
You can find more information in No. 11 Succulents and Moss Arrangement on page 140

arrange22
シシゴケ、センペルビューム

Design 22
Shishigoke (*Brothera leana*)
Sempervivum

arrange23
ホソバオキナゴケ
サボテン (キンコウマル)
サボテン (コガネツカサ)

Design 23
Hosobaokinagoke
(*Leucobryum juniperoideum*)
Kinkoumaru cactus
(*Parodia leninghausii*)
Koganetsukasa
(*Mammillaria elongate*)

arrange24
シシゴケ
多肉植物 (エケベリア)

Design 24
Shishigoke (*Brothera leana*)
Succulent (*Echeveria*)

arrange 25　グラスの中のピンクリーフトゥリー　　　　　Design 25. Pink Leaf Tree in a Glass
arrange 26　紅実のカルテット　　　　　　　　　　　　Design 26. Quartet of Red Berries

少し形の異なるガラスに、コケモモとコケを寄せ植えしました。
　実がなっていたり、斑が入っているかで雰囲気も違う作品になります。
　グラスの底にはゼオライトを入れ、水が溜まらないように管理します。また、中心を高く植えるとコケも良く見え美しいです。

I planted mosses together with *Vaccinium vitis-idaea* L. in two glassware shaped differently. If you add berries or variegated leaves, it creates a different look. I put zeolite on the bottom of the glassware to eliminate the accumulation of water. Try to plant it higher in the center, because it makes the moss look even more beautiful.

グラスに、白い花が爽やかなヤシュウハナゼキショウと、紅い実がたわわに実ったニシベツコケモモ、それにホソバオキナゴケを寄せ植えしました。ホソウリゴケは飛び込みです。

I planted white flowered *Tofieldia furusei*, red berries of *Vaccinium*, and *Leucobryum juniperoideum*. Then the *Brachymenium exile* joined by itself.

arrange26
ホソバオキナゴケ、ホソウリゴケ、
ニシベツコケモモ、ヤシュウハナゼキショウ

Design 26
Hosobaokinagoke (*Leucobryum juniperoideum*)
Hosourigoke (*Brachymenium exile*)
Nishibetsukokemomo (*Vaccinium vitis-idaea* L.)
Yashuhanazekisho (*Tofieldia furusei*)

arrange25
ホソバオキナゴケ、斑入りコケモモ

Design 25
Hosobaokinagoke (*Leucobryum juniperoideum*)
Fuiri kokemomo (*vaiegated Vaccinum vitis-idaea* L.)

グラスに、芽出しがピンク色で可愛い斑入りコケモモと、ホソバオキナゴケをアレンジしました。斑入りのコケモモは果実にも縞々の斑が入ります。

Planted *V. vitis-idaea* of pink variegated leaves and *L. juniperoideum*. The variegated variety also has striped berries.

arrange 27 卓上のクリスマス Design 27. Christmas on the Desk

陶器の植木鉢に、クリスマスアレンジ。斑入りツルマサキ、ヒメヒイラギを使い、ホソバオキナゴケを根元に植え緑の絨毯に。ヒメヒイラギはヒイラギと違いモチノキ科で、在来種では珍しい本当のクリスマスホーリーです。飾り付けをしてお部屋で楽しみましょう。

I made an arrangement of Christmas by planting *Euonymus fortune* variegate and *Ilex dimorphophylla*, and then adding *Leucobryum juniperoideum* to create a green carpet. Ilex is true holy for Christmas, and it is native in Japan. I arranged it with some seasonal decoration to enhance the atmosphere.

arrange27
ホソバオキナゴケ、斑入りツルマサキ
アマミヒイラギモチ (ヒメヒイラギ)

Design 27
Hosobaokinagoke (*Leucobryum juniperoideum*), Fuiri tsurumaki (*Variagated Euonymus fortunei*) and Amamihiiragimochi (*Ilex dimorphophylla*)

arrange 28　ココットの中の雪山　　　　　　　　　Design 28. Snow Mountain in a Cocotte Plate

　少し大きなココット皿にシモフリゴケを使い、雪山イメージしアレンジしました。シモフリゴケは乾くと、まるで粉雪が降り積もったかのように、真っ白に変わります。乾いた時を楽しむコケもあります。

In a bigger cocotte plate, I planted *Rhacomitrium lanuginosum* as an image of a snow mountain. When it is dry, it turns white as if it is covered with powdered snow. It is a rare moss to enjoy when it's dry.

arrange28
シモフリゴケ

Design 28
Shimofurigoke (*Rhacomitrium lanuginosum*)

arrange 29 ディープフォレスト

Design 29. Deep Forest

　小さな水槽に、珍しいコケをたくさん使い深山をレイアウトしました。
　ヤシの木のようなコウヤノマンネングサや番傘のようなオオカサゴケは一本でも十分インパクトのある姿です。そのコケを複数使うことで、まるで樹海のようです。
　初めにサンゴを飼育するタンクのような岩組をしてからコケを植えていきます。
タンクサイズ　300㎜×200㎜×250㎜ (H)

In a small sized tank, I used many rare species to create a deep forest. A palm tree-like *Cimacium japaonicum* and an umbrella-like *Rhodobryum giganteum* created a sea of trees. First of all, you need to make the rock formation of breeding the coral. Then, plant mosses on it. The tank size is 300mm×200mm×250mm (H).

arrange29
コウヤノマンネングサ、
ホソバオキナゴケ、ネズミノオゴケ、
オオカサゴケ、ウマスギゴケ、
コツボゴケ、ジャゴケ、
ヒメミヤマウズラ

Design 29
Kouyanomannengusa (*Cimacium japaonicum*)
Hosobaokinagoke (*Leucobryum juniperoideum*)
Nezuminoogoke (*Myuroclada maximowiczii*)
Ookasagoke (*Rhodobryum giganteum*)
Kotsubogoke (*Plagiomnium acutum*)
Umasugigoke (*Polytrichum commune*)
Jagoke (*Conocephalum conicum*)
Himemiyamauzura (*Gooduera repens*)

arrange 30　ヤンバルの森
arrange 31　水底を覗くと
arrange 32　森のせせらぎの音

arrange30
トヤマシノブゴケ
コツボゴケ、タマゴケ
ホソバミズゼニゴケ
ウマスギゴケ、チャセンシダ

Design 30
Forest of Yanbar
Toyamashinobugoke
(*Thuidium kanedae*)
Kotsubogoke (*Plagiomnium acutum*)
Tamagoke (*Bartramia pomiformis*)
Hosobamizuzenigoke (*Pellia endivifolia*)
Umasugigoke (*Polytrichum commune*)
Chasenshida (*Asplenium trichomanes*)

　真っ白なサンゴ岩とサンゴ砂を使い、真っ青な空のもとに広がる森をイメージして作りました。
タンクサイズ 450㎜× 200㎜× 250㎜ (H)

I created this with white, coral leaf-rocks and coral sands, which created an image of a forest under the blue sky in a tropical island. The tank size is 450mm x 200mm x 250mm.

　日本の森の、爽やかな風が通る清流をイメージし作りました。タンクサイズ 1200㎜× 450㎜× 450㎜ (H)

110

Design 30. Forest of Yanbar
Design 31. Look into the Depth of Water
Design 32. The Sound of Little Stream in the Woods

arrange31
コケ類：ヤナギゴケ、ミズキャラゴケ
　　　　ツルチョウチンゴケ
水草類：エビモ、スブタ、フサモ
　　　　オオカナダモ、コカナダモ
魚　類：シロメダカ
　　　　アルビノコメット (金魚)
　　　　アルビノバラタナゴ

Design 31
Look into the Depth of Water
Mosses : Yanagigoke (*Fontinalis antipyretica*)
　　Mizukyaragoke (*Taxiphyllum Barbieri*)
　　Tsurucyouchingoke
　　　(*Plagiomnium maximoviczii*)
Water plant : Ebimo (*Potamogeton crispus*)
　　Subuta (*Blyxa echinosperma*)
　　Fusamo (*Myriophyllus*)
　　Ookanadamo (*Egeria densa*)
　　Kokanadamo (*Elodia nuttallii*)
Fishes : Shiro medaka (*white Oryzias latipes*),
　　Albino kingyo (*albino commet Carassius auratus auratus*),
　　Albino nipponbaratanago (*albino Rhodeus ocellatus kurumeus*)

水草がそよぎ、透き通った水が、こんこんと湧く泉をイメージして作りました。
タンクサイズ
450㎜× 300㎜× 300㎜ (H)

I designed it with the image of transparent and abundant spring water. The tank size is 450 mm x 300 mm x 300 mm (H).

This is the image of a clear Japanese stream.　The tank size is 1200mm x 450mm x 450mm (H).

arrange32
ハイゴケ、トヤマシノブゴケ
ヒメシノブゴケ、ナルコスゲ
カンスゲ、タマアジサイ
ホトトギス、イワタバコ
シノブ、ジュウモンジシダ
イワデンダ、トリアシショウマ

Design 32
The Sound of Little Stream in the Woods
Haigoke (*Hypnum plumaeforme*)
Toyamashinobugoke (*Thuidium kanedae*)
Himeshinobugoke (*T.cymbifolium*)
Narukosuge (*Carex curvivicollis*)
Kansuge (*C.morrowii*)
Tamaajisai (*Hydrangea involuvrata*)
Hototogisu (*Coculus poliocephalus*)
Iwatabako (*Canandron ramondioides*)
Shinbone (*Davallia mariesii*)
Juumonjishida (*Polystichum tripteron*)
Iwadenda (*Woodsia polystichoides*)
Toriashisyouma (*Astilbe odontophylla*)

111

arrange 33 「人研ぎ流し」に作る苔の箱庭

　人研ぎ流しは昭和の時代にはどこの庭先にもありました。しかし、今はあまり見かけなくなりました。
　その流しは人工石でできています。素材の石は夏の温度上昇を緩やかにし、また溜まった熱を放熱してくれます。
　そんなレトロでも機能性に優れた人研ぎ流しに、小さな苔の箱庭を作りました。溶岩を使い少し起伏を出し、紫色の花を集め。涼しげで爽やかな感じに仕上げました。
　詳しい作り方はP142に、わかりやすく紹介しています。

Design 33 A Miniature Moss Garden in the Sink

arrange33
トヤマシノブゴケ、ハイゴケ、ベニチガヤ、ヒメヤバネススキ、カンスゲ、ナミキソウ、ソバナ、アオバナホタルブクロ、ミヤマウグイスカグラ、ヒメウツギ、イワヒバ、カタヒバ

Design 33
Toyamashinobugoke (*Thuidium kanedae*)   Haigoke (*Hypnum plumaeforme*)
Benichigaya (*Imperata cylindrica*)   Himeyabanesusuki (*Miscanthus sinensis 'Zebrinus'*)   Kansuge (*Carexmorrowii*)   Namikisou (*Scutellaria strigillosa*)   Sobana (*Adenophora remotiflora*) Aobanahotarubukuro (*Enkianthus quinqueflorus*)
Miyamauguisukagura (*Lonicera gracilipes*)   Himeutsugi (*Deutzia gracilis*)
Iwahiba (*Selaginella tamariscina*)   Katahiba(*Selaginella tamariscina*)

This is an old-fashioned water sink made out of artificial stone. It can be radiant hot in the summer, so to prevent the temperature rising, I used lava rocks to make undulation. I created a miniature moss garden with purple wild flowers to make a refreshing feeling.
Reference is No. 12. Moss terrarium in Japanese Sink made by an artificial stone (P142) You can find the easy manual.

arrange 34 石板の上のオアシス　　　　　　　　　　　　　　Design 34 Oasis on a Stone Plate

ヤマアジサイやエゾアジサイは日本の深山に自生しています。日陰で涼しく、湿度のある場所を好みます。
　鉢植えや庭植えでも楽しめますが、苔玉もまた風情があります。
　今回は石板に固定した、苔玉風のアレンジにしました。
　詳しい作り方はP134に、わかりやすく紹介しています。

Hydrangea serrata and *H.s.var megacarpa* are native in the depths of the mountains in Japan. They prefer moisture and can be enjoyed in pots and gardens. However, a moss ball is another option. I tried to put it on the stone plate similar to a moss ball. Reference is No.8 *Hydrangea serrata* Moss Ball on stone board (See P134).

arrange34
トヤマシノブゴケ、ヤマアジサイ

Design 34
Toyamashinobugoke (*Thuidium kanedae*)
Yamaajisai (*Hydrangea serrata*)

arrange 35　ガラスの中のジャングル　　　　　　　　　Design 35 The Jungle in a Glass Jar

食虫植物のサラセニアは北アメリカの湿地帯に自生しています。水枯れに弱いため鉢植えでは、鉢底を水の張った容器に浸けて栽培する腰水栽培をします。

ここではデザートグラスにコツボゴケといっしょにアレンジしました。

詳しい作り方はP132に、わかりやすく紹介しています。

A Sarracenia is a carnivorous plant native in the wetland of North America. It is vulnerable to dry conditions, and you can grow them in the waist water method. In this method you can put a pot into a shallow container and fill it with water. I planted it in a dessert glass with *Plagiomnium actum*. Reference is in No. 7 Carnivorous plant and Moss terrarium (P132)

arrange35
コツボゴケ、サラセニア

Design 35
Kotsubogoke (*Plagiomnium actum*)
Sarracenia

115

arrange 36　ファレノプシスとコケの浮遊アレンジ　　　Design 36 Blooming in the Air Phalaenopsis and Moss

ファレノプシス(胡蝶蘭)は東南アジアの熱帯、亜熱帯のジャングルの中の高い木に着生しています。
　そのため、鉢植えでなくても栽培できます。
　コーヒーフィルタースタンドにトヤマシノブゴケとファレノプシスを使いアレンジしました。
　詳しい作り方はP136に、わかりやすく紹介しています。

Phalaenopsis dwells epiphytically on the tall trees in the sub-tropical and tropical climates of South East Asia. You can grow them without a plant pot. I made it in a coffee filter and planted it together with *Thuidium kanedae*. Reference is No. 9 Blooming-in-the-air Phalaenopsis and Moss Terrarium (P136)

arrange36
トヤマシノブゴケ、ファレノプシス、マメヅタ

Design 36
Toyamashinobugoke (*Thuidium kanedae*)
Phalaenopsis, Mamezuta (*Lemmaphyllum microphyllum*)

arrange 37　ガラスの中の宝石　　　　　　　　　　Design 37 Precious Stone in a Glass

　蓋付きのガラスの容器に、コツボゴケとベニシュスランを植えました。ベニシュスランは日本の深山に生える野生ランです。
　この種類のランは、葉に宝石のように美しい模様があることからジュエルオーキッドと呼ばれています。ベニシュスランもそのうちの一つです。ベニシュスランは花も美しくピンク色の花を7月頃咲かせます。
　暗く湿った環境が好きなランなので、コツボゴケとは相性が良いのです。
　作品を作るコツは、ランの根が折れやすいので、これを折らないように気をつけガラスの容器に入れることです。

In a container with a lid, I have planted *Plagiomnium acutum* and *Goodyera biflora*, which is a native wild orchid growing in the mountains of Japan. It is called a Jewel Orchid, because the beautiful foliage looks like jewels. It has pretty pink flowers that last for 7 months. It prefers dark and moist places, and it looks so happy with *P.acutum*. The roots of orchids are easy to break, so try not to damage them.

arrange37
コツボゴケ、ベニシュスラン

Design 37
Kotsubogoke (*Plagiomnium acutum*)
Benisyusuran (*Goodyera biflora*)

117

arrange 38 頭上の花園　　　　　　　　　　　　Design 38 Airy Flower Garden

野生でのカトレアは中南米の熱帯や亜熱帯に多く、ジャングルの中で高く生い茂った木の幹に根を這わせ、くっついています。

容器に植えるのではなく、今回は流木にカトレアを植えつけます。

その姿を想像し、ミニカトレアとホソバオキナゴケを使いアレンジしました。

詳しい作り方はP138に、わかりやすく紹介しています。

Cattleya is native in Latin America's tropical and sub-tropical regions. It inhabits crawling on the trunks of vigorous trees. I chose to plant it on drifted wood instead of a pot, along with Mini Cattleya and *Leucobryum juniperoideum*. Reference is No. 10 Miniature Cattleya blooming on an Old Tree（P138）

arrange38
ホソバオキナゴケ、ミニカトレア " ヤマブキ "

Design 38
Hosobaokinagoke (*Leucobryum juniperoideum*)
Mini Cattleya (Yamabuki)

HOW TO

いろいろなタイプの
コケリウムの作り方を
わかりやすく解説

An easy and basic
introduction of how to
make moss terrarium
gardens

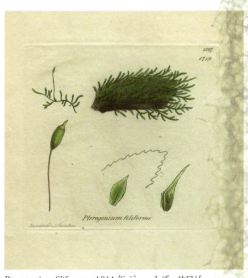

Pterogonium filiforme　1811年 ジェームズ・サワビー

1　手を汚さず簡単に作れる苔玉

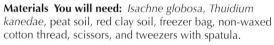

チゴザサを使って、涼しげな苔玉を作ります。
苔玉は作り方によっては何年も楽しむことができます。
あまり手を汚さず簡単に作れ、
長持ちする苔玉を作りましょう。
ロウ加工してない木綿糸を使うことで
すぐに糸が腐り、見えなくなります。

Use *Isachne globosa* (Chigozasa) to make a refreshing moss ball. If you make them in a specific way then you can enjoy handmade ones for years. Let me show you how to make long lasting moss balls without getting your hands too dirty. I recommend using non-waxed cotton thread, because it rots and disappears quickly.

用意するもの　チゴザサ、トヤマシノブゴケ、ケト土、硬質赤玉土小粒、フリーザーパック、ロウ加工してない木綿糸、ハサミ、ヘラ付きピンセット

Materials You will need: *Isachne globosa*, *Thuidium kanedae*, peat soil, red clay soil, freezer bag, non-waxed cotton thread, scissors, and tweezers with spatula.

1 Easy to make moss balls

1　フリーザーパックにケト土、硬質赤玉土小粒、水を入れて混ぜます。から揚げの衣くらいの硬さ。
2　チゴザサをポットから抜き、フリーザーパックの中に入れます。
3　トヤマシノブゴケを正方形にハサミで切ります。
4　チゴザサの根鉢の周りに、まんべんなく用土が付いたら取り出します。
5　用土は薄く付くくらいで大丈夫です。用土はコケとの接着剤になります。
6　トヤマシノブゴケを裏返して仮根側にし、中央に乗せます。
7　トヤマシノブゴケの四隅を持ち上げて包みます。横にして置き、糸で1周して固結びにします。
8　片手に乗せて何回か糸を巻きます。横に巻いたら縦にも何回か巻きます。
9　最後に横に巻き、始めに固結びした糸に結びます。ハサミで糸を切ります。
10　コケをハサミで切り、形を整えて完成です。水をたっぷり与えてお皿の上に置いて管理します。朝、お皿に水を入れ、夜にはなくなるくらいが適量です。半日陰で管理します。

1. Put peat soil, red clay soil, and water into a freezer bag and mix together. The consistency should be like the batter of fish and chips.
2. Pull out *Isachne globosa* from a pot and put it into the freezer bag.
3. Cut *Thuidium kanedae* into square shapes.
4. When the soil is evenly attached around the root pot, take out *I. globosa* from the freezer bag.
5. The amount of soil that is attached to the root pot doesn't need to be thick, because this soil becomes an adhesive with moss.
6. Turn *Thuidium kanedae* upside down on the temporary root side and place it in the center.
7. Lift up the four corners of *Thuidium kanedae* and wrap and tie it with a thread.
8. Put it on one of your hands and wind the thread. After winding horizontally several times, do the same vertically.
9. Finally, tie the end of the thread that you are holding to the other side of it where you started to wind horizontally. Cut the thread with scissors.
10. Arrange the shape of your moss with scissors to complete it, and give it plenty of water and place it on a plate. When you water it in the morning, the water should be gone at night. This indicates that it is the appropriate amount of water. Make sure to keep your moss in the shade.

2　水が好きな苔を使ったコケリウム

オオカサゴケやコツボゴケは見た目が美しいコケですが、非常に乾燥に弱い種類です。
周りに水を張ることで容器内の空気湿度を保て、コケが傷まなくなります。

Rhodobryum giganteum and *Plagiomnium acutum* are beautiful moss, yet they are very vulnerable to dryness. You can maintain the air humidity by pouring water around the moss. This also protects it from being damaged.

用意するもの　オオカサゴケ、コツボゴケ、硬質赤玉土小粒、ガラス砂、ガラス容器、ヘラ付きピンセット、霧吹き、用土入れ

Materials You will need: *Rhodobryum giganteum*, *Plagiomnium acutum*, red clay soil, glass sand, tweezers with spatula, sprayer, and soil container.

2 Water-loving Moss Terrarium

1　二重ガラス容器の中央に、硬質赤玉土小粒を入れる。
2　オオカサゴケを中央にまとめて持ち、周りをコツボゴケで包み込みます。コツボゴケが重ならない量をハサミで切り取ります。
3　指先で整えます。
4　オオカサゴケの下にコツボゴケがあるような配置にします。
5　ピンセットで持ちます。
6　中央の硬質赤玉土小粒を入れた上に乗せます。
7　コケが、外側の容器の縁より出ないようにします。
8　ガラス容器の内側に、ガラス砂をヘラで入れていきます。
9　底全体にガラス砂を入れます。
10　コケに霧吹きし、ガラス砂が水で浸かるまで水を入れて完成です。

日の当たらない室内で管理します。つねにガラス砂が水に浸かっているように、ときどき水を入れます。

1. Put Red clay soil in the center of a double-layered glass container.
2. Hold *Rhodobryum giganteum* in the middle and wrap around it with *Plagiomnium acutum*. Cut some overlapped parts of P. acutum with scissors.
3. Shape it well with your fingers.
4. Place *P. acutu* under the *R. giganteum*.
5. Hold it with tweezers.
6. Put it on top of the red clay soil.
7. Make sure the moss does not protrude from the edge of the outer layer of the container.
8. Using a spatula, put glass sand into the bottom of the glass container.
9. Fill the bottom of the outer layer of the glass container with glass sand.
10. Complete by spraying the moss and pouring water on the glass sand until it's covered.

Keep this moss terrarium indoors and in the shade. Also, make sure the glass sand is always covered by the water.

3　上からも横からも見える。ボトルシップ型コケリウム

ガラスボトルのコケリウムは
横から見るものが多いです。
それは、製作の過程で上からコケや石を
入れて作るからです。
でもこのコケリウムは上からも覗けます。

Many glass bottle moss terrariums are designed to be seen from the sides. This is because we lay out moss and stones looking inside the container from the top. However, this Ship-in-a-bottle style Moss terrarium that I'm going to introduce, can be enjoyed from both sides, as well as from above.

用意するもの　ネズミノオゴケ、コツボゴケ、オオカサゴケ、硬質赤玉土小粒、石、砂利、ガラスボトル、ヘラ付きピンセット、ハサミ、用土入れ

Materials You will need: *Myuroclada maximowiczii, Plagiomnium acutum, Rhodobryum giganteum*, red clay soil, stones, gravel, glass bottle, tweezers with spatula, scissors and soil container.

124

3 Ship-in-a-bottle style Moss terrarium that you can enjoy from any angle

1　ガラスボトルに硬質赤玉土小粒を蓋の口下くらいまで入れます。奥のほうは多く入れ、傾斜をつけます。
2　石を入れます。石はガラスが傷つかないように角のないものを使います。
3　上から作れないので、ボトルシップ型は中を6分割にして奥から一箇所ずつ完成させていきます。ピンセットと指で6分割を示しました。
4　ハサミでネズミノオゴケを切ります。
5　奥から、切ったネズミノオゴケをピンセットで挟み入れていきます。
6　入り口のパーツは、カタカナのコの字になるようにハサミで切ります。
7　ピンセットで挟み入れます。
8　オオカサゴケをピンセットで挟み、石の脇に入れます。ピンセットでいくつかの砂利をつまみ、オオカサゴケの元に入れ押さえます。
9　蓋側から中を見たところ。
10　水をボトルの口から入れます。
11　何回か、水の濁りがなくなるまで水を入れ替えます。
12　ピンセットにキッチンペーパーを巻き、ボトルの内側の水滴を丁寧に拭き完成です。

1. Put red clay soil inside, and the thickness of the soil should be just below the entrance of the bottle. Add more soil in the bottom and place it diagonally.
2. Add some stones. Make sure to use round stones, not edgy ones because this could damage your glass bottle.
3. As we can't layout from the top, let's divide the area into 6 parts and complete the sections one by one starting from the bottom. I'm showing how the area is divided by using tweezers with my fingers.
4. Cut *Myuroclada maximowiczii*.
5. Start putting *M. maximowiczii* in the bottom of the bottle.
6. Cut another piece of M. maximowiczii into a 'U' shape. This will be placed near the mouth of bottle.
7. Use tweezers to lay everything out.
8. Take *Rhodobryum giganteum* with tweezers and set it a part from the stone. Add some gravel on *R. giganteum* to make it stay still.
9. View from the mouth of the bottle side.
10. Pour some water into the bottle.
11. Repeatedly water and pour out several times, so that the water becomes clear.
12. Wrap tweezers with a paper towel and wipe the inside of the bottle to make it completely clean.

4 ガラスドームにコケの生えた岩山を再現したコケリウム

もともとはポプリ入れのガラスドームです。
ガラスが薄いので取り扱いは注意が必要です。
ドーム型で蓋をすれば湿度が保たれ、
コケも綺麗です。

Originally this glass dome is used for displaying potpourri. This kind of container tends to be a delicate layer of glass, so please take extra care when you use them. Covering the terrarium with a dome holds the humidity and keeps the moss beautiful.

用意するもの　ナガバチヂレゴケ、ノミハニワゴケ、溶岩、硬質赤玉土小粒、純度100パーセントのシアノアクリレート系ボンド、ヘラ付きピンセット、ハサミ、霧吹き、用土入れ

Materials You will need: *Ptychomitrium linearifolium, Haplocladium angustifolium*, lava, red clay soil, 100% pure super glue cyanoacrylate adhesive, tweezers with spatula, scissors, sprayer, and soil container.

4 Rocky Mountain style Moss Terrarium in a glass dome

1 ハサミで、ドームの直径に合わせノミハニワゴケを切り取ります。ドームの受け側の容器に、硬質赤玉土小粒を入れます。
2 硬質赤玉土小粒の上に、ノミハニワゴケを敷きます。ピンセットを使い、縁の近くのコケを立たせます。
3 ナガバチヂレゴケを小さな円形に整えます。
4 溶岩のどこに付けるか位置をを決めます。
5 溶岩に接している仮根を持ち上げて、ボンドを溶岩に付けます。仮根を押し当てて付けます。
6 ピンセットで整えます。
7 コケを敷いたドームの受け側に溶岩を乗せます。
8 霧吹きをして全体を湿らせた状態にします。
9 ドームをかぶせて完成です。気温が高いと傷むため、なるべく涼しい場所で管理します。乾いてきたら全体に霧吹きをします。

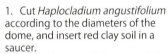

1. Cut *Haplocladium angustifolium* according to the diameters of the dome, and insert red clay soil in a saucer.
2. Place *H. angustifolium* in red clay soil. Use tweezers to pull up some moss on the edges.
3. Make *Ptychomitrium linearifolium* into a round shape.
4. Decide what part of the lava you will place the moss.
5. Lift up the temporary root and use the adhesive to stick it on the lava.
6. Use tweezers to shape it.
7. Put lava on the saucer.
8. Spray water over the moss to moisturize it.
9. Complete by covering the saucer with a dome. Keep this terrarium in a cool place, because it is easily damaged by heat. When it's dry, spray water again on it.

127

5 紫水晶とコケのハーモニーを楽しむコケリウム

用意するもの コツボゴケ、硬質赤玉土小粒、麦飯石、紫水晶、ガラスの容器、ヘラ付きピンセット、ハサミ、霧吹き、用土入れ

Materials You will need: *Plagiomnium acutum*, red clay soil, Maifan stone, purple crystal, glass container, tweezers with spatula, scissors, spray bottle, and soil container.

5 Purple Crystal Moss Terrarium

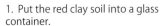

1　容器に硬質赤玉土小粒を入れます。
2　入る大きさにハサミで切ります。
3　ピンセットで挟み、コツボゴケを入れます。
4　コツボゴケを紫水晶で挟まないように、手で避けながら入れます。
5　ピンセットで整えます。
6　紫水晶とコツボゴケの周りに硬質赤玉土小粒を入れます。
7　平らになるようにヘラで均します。
8　紫水晶を揺らし、隙間にも硬質赤玉土小粒が入るようにします。
9　麦飯石をピンセットで摘み並べていきます。
10　なるべく硬質赤玉土小粒が見えないように麦飯石を入れます。
11　霧吹きをして全体を湿らせます。硬質赤玉土小粒の色が濃くなるのが目安です。
12　キッチンペーパーでガラス容器の内側を拭き、蓋をして完成です。

1. Put the red clay soil into a glass container.
2. Cut *Plagiomnium acutum* and place it into a container.
3. Use tweezers to place the moss.
4. Put purple crystal into the container without damaging the moss.
5. Shape well with the tweezers.
6. Put red clay soil around the moss and crystal.
7. Use the spatula to make the soil flat.
8. Shake the crystal a little, so the soil can get into the small gaps.
9. Place Maifan stones inside with the tweezers.
10. Try to cover the soil with Maifan stones as much as you can.
11. Spray water over the terrarium. When the red clay soil turns a darker color, it has an appropriate amount of humidity.
12. Use the paper towel to wipe the inside of the glass container. and set a lid on top to complete the creation.

6 オオカサゴケと縞々石のコケリウム

オオカサゴケはまるで番傘が開いたような姿です。このオオカサゴケを縞模様の石と合わせ、ガラス容器の中にじっくり観察できる小さな林を作りました。

R. giganteum looks like an open umbrella. Let's create the woods in a glass container by using the moss and striped patterned stones.

用意するもの オオカサゴケ、硬質赤玉土小粒、石、砂利、ガラスの容器、ピンセット、ハサミ、霧吹き、用土入れ

Materials You will need: *Rhodobryum giganteum*, red clay soil, stones, gravel, glass container, tweezers, scissors, sprayer, and soil container.

6 Rhodobryum giganteum and striped pattern stone Moss Terrarium

1　ガラス容器に硬質赤玉土小粒を入れます。
2　オオカサゴケは葉より下の1次体が長いため、少し厚めに敷きます。
3　ピンセットで1本ずつ埋めていきます。
4　1次体が埋まれば、少し斜めになっても石を入れてから修正できます。
5　中央に縞模様の石を入れます。
6　ピンセットでオオカサゴケの角度を整えます。
7　いくつか小さめの石を入れます。
8　入れたらピンセットで整えます。
9　石を入れた状態。
10　周りに砂利を入れます。
11　ピンセットで砂利を並べていきます。
12　霧吹きをして全体を湿らせ、内側をキッチンペーパーで拭きます。蓋をして完成です。

2日に一回くらい霧吹きをしてオオカサゴケを湿らせます。

1. Put red clay soil into the glass container.
2. The layer of soil should be thicker like *Rhodobryum giganteum,* because it has a long primary root system below the leaves.
3. Put roots one after another into the soil by using tweezers.
4. As long as the primary root system is in the soil, you can fix the angle later when placing the stones.
5. Position the striped pattern stones in the center.
6. Adjust the angle of the moss by using tweezers.
7. Add some small stones.
8. Adjust the position of stones with tweezers.
9. View after placing the stones.
10. Add gravel around it.
11. Use tweezers to place the gravel.
12. Spray water to moisturize, and then wipe inside the glass container with a paper towel. Set a lid on top to complete the creation.
Spray water on it once every two days.

7　食虫植物とコケのアレンジ

食虫植物のサラセニアをデザートグラスに入れ、
コツボゴケを使いアレンジしました。
水の好きなコケと植物の組み合わせです。

I planted a carnivorous plant called Sarracenia, in a dessert glass bowl alongside *Plagiomnium acutum*. This is a nice combination layout of water-loving moss and plants.

用意するもの　コツボゴケ、サラセニア、硬質赤玉土、ガラスの器、ピンセット、ハサミ、用土入れ

Materials You will need: *Plagiomnium acutum*, Sarracenia, red clay soil, dessert glass bowl, tweezers, spatula, scissors, and soil container.

7 Carnivorous plant and Moss terrarium

1　ガラスの器に硬質赤玉土小粒を入れます。
2　器の半分くらいまで入れます。
3　サラセニアをポットから抜き、根の周りの用土を取り除きます。
4　中央にサラセニアを置きます。
5　サラセニアを押さえながら、周りに硬質赤玉土小粒を入れます。
6　器の中央が高くなるように硬質赤玉土小粒を入れます。
7　コケシートの半分のところを手で持ち、コケシートの中心まで裂きます。
8　サラセニアの周りにかぶせます。
9　かぶせた状態。
10　ヘラの裏面を使い、コケの縁を器に押し入れていきます。
11　片手でコケと器を押さえ、器を少しずつ回しながらヘラの裏面でコケを器に押し入れていきます。
12　ピンセットでコケを挟みます。
13　サラセニアの根元の隙間にピンセットでコケを入れていきます。
14　ヘラで整えます。
15　全体をシャワーで洗い流して完成です。

1. Put the red clay soil into a dessert glass bowl.
2. Fill up half of the bowl with soil.
3. Take out Sarracenia from the pot and remove the soil around the roots.
4. Place Sarracenia in the center.
5. Insert the red clay soil while holding Sarracenia straight.
6. Add more soil in the center to make it higher.
7. Hold the moss sheet and tear in the middle.
8. Cover the foot of Sarracenia with the moss.
9. View after covering the soil.
10. Use the back of the spatula and gently press down the edges of the moss into the bowl.
11. Hold and turn the bowl around, while pressing the moss down.
12. Take some moss with tweezers.
13. Add the moss to the foot of Sarracenia.
14. Shape it with a spatula.
15. Rinse it with a shower of water to complete.

8 石板に乗るヤマアジサイのコケ山

まるで石板に乗せた苔玉のような、
石板と一体型のヤマアジサイとコケのアレンジです。
苔玉より作りやすく、管理も簡単です。

This arrangement is made with *Hydrangea serrata* and moss integrated with a stone board. Compared to a normal moss ball, this is easier to make and take care of.

用意するもの トヤマシノブゴケ、ヤマアジサイ、湿らせた硬質赤玉土小粒、石板、アルミ線、エポキシ樹脂接着剤、ヘラ付きピンセット、ハサミ
＊あらかじめ石板にアルミ線を2液性エポキシ樹脂接着剤で固定させておきます。

Materials You will need: *Thuidium kanedae*, *Hydrangea serrata*, moistened red clay soil, stone board, aluminum wire, Epoxy resin adhesive, tweezers with a spatula, and scissors.
*In advance, glue the aluminum wire to the stone board with epoxy resin adhesive.

8 Hydrangea serrata Moss Ball on Stone board

1　ヤマアジサイをポットから抜き、上部の用土を削り落とします。コケを貼った時丸みを出すため。
2　固定してあるアルミ線に、ヤマアジサイを少し斜めにして刺し通します。
3　アルミ線の先を曲げ、ヤマアジサイの根元に刺します。
4　横にしてヤマアジサイが固定されているか確認します。
5　石板に固定したヤマアジサイ。
6　湿らせた硬質赤玉土小粒を、ヤマアジサイの用土全体に乗せていきます。
7　なるべく高く乗せます。仕上がりが綺麗になります。
8　トヤマシノブゴケのシートをハサミで長方形に切ります。
9　ヤマアジサイの根元をコケシートで巻きます。
10　長すぎたら、余分なコケシートをハサミで切ります。
11　ヘラの裏面を使い、コケシートを石板と根元の隙間に押し入れていきます。
12　余分なコケを切り整えます。
13　ヘラの裏面で再度整えます。
14　シャワーでたっぷり水を与えて完成です。
石板が浸かるくらいの浅いお皿に飾り、水を張り、直射日光の当たらない半日陰で管理します。

1. Take out the *Hydrangea serrata* from the pot and scrape off the top part of the soil to shape it into a round ball; a moss ball.
2. Diagonally pierce through the hydrangea with a fixed aluminum wire.
3. Bend the aluminum wire and pierce the foot of the root of hydrangea.
4. Lift up the stone board and make sure hydrangea is attached well.
5. View hydrangea attached to the stone board.
6. Cover up the soil of hydrangea with the moistened red clay soil.
7. Put the red clay soil as high as possible, so it looks beautiful.
8. Cut a sheet of *Thuidium kanedae* in a rectangular shape.
9. Wrap the foot of the plant with a moss sheet.
10. If the sheet is too long, trim the unwanted parts with scissors.
11. Use the back of the spatula to press in the moss sheet into the gap between the stone board and the soil.
12. Trim the unwanted parts of moss again.
13. Shape it again using the spatula.
14. Shower it with plenty of water to finish. Decorate it on a shallow plate, so the stone board can be emerged when you fill it with water. Keep it in a partly shady area, away from direct sunlight.

9 ファレノプシスとコケの浮遊アレンジ

ファレノプシスやデンドロビウムなど着生タイプのランは、もともとは樹上に生えています。
コーヒーフィルタースタンドにコケを使ってバスケットを作り、空中に咲いた姿をイメージしアレンジしました。

Orchids like Phalaenopsis and Dendrobium inhabit on trees. I designed a basket style terrarium using a coffee filter stand and placed it by the Orchids blooming in the air.

用意するもの トヤマシノブゴケ、マメヅタ、ファレノプシス、スチールスタンド、ヘラ付きピンセット、ハサミ

Materials You will need: *Thuidium kanedae, Lemmaphyllum microphyllum,* Phalaenopsis, a steel coffee filter stand, tweezers with spatula, and scissors.

9 Blooming in the air Phalaenopsis and Moss Terrarium

1　トヤマシノブゴケにマメヅタを植え栽培した大きめのシートを裏返して用意します。
2　スタンドの内側に入れます。
3　スタンドの形状に沿って、隙間のないように押し当てます。
4　側面から、穴や隙間がないか確認します。
5　入れたコケシートの縁を外側に開きます。
6　ファレノプシスを鉢から抜きます。
7　根鉢を崩さないまま、コケのバスケットの中に入れます。
8　縁のコケシートをファレノプシスの根元にかぶせます。
9　なるべく根元全体を包みます。
10　ピンセットで重なる部分を整えます。
11　挟まっているマメヅタやトヤマシノブゴケをピンセットで引っ張り出します。
12　シャワーでたっぷり水を与えて完成です。

日の当たらない明るい窓辺で管理します。3日に1回蛇口からたっぷり水を与えます。

1. Plant *Lemmaphyllum microphyllum* on a large sheet of cultivated *Thuidium kanedae*, and then turn it over.
2. Put it inside the coffee filter stand.
3. Press gently according to the shape of stand to make sure no crevice remains.
4. Turn it around and check that there are no holes or gaps.
5. Open the edge of the outer moss sheet.
6. Take out Phalaenopsis from the pot.
7. Place it in the stand without breaking the root clump.
8. Cover the foot of Phalaenopsis with the moss from the edges.
9. Wrap as much of the root as possible.
10. Adjust the overlapped part of moss with tweezers.
11. Pull out *L. microphyllum* and *T. kanedae*.
12. Shower with plenty of water to complete the process.
Keep it by the bright windowsill, but not in direct sunlight. Water it from the faucet once every 3 days.

10 古木に咲くミニカトレアをイメージしたアレンジ

形のよい流木にホソバオキナゴケを
ボンドで張り合わせ、コケの器を作り、
カトレアを使い
野趣あふれるアレンジを作りました。

I glued *Leucobryum neilgherrense* on beautiful driftwood and used it as a base. It created an enchanting and rustic beauty.

用意するもの ホソバオキナゴケ、ミニカトレア、流木、純度100パーセントのシアノアクリレート系ボンド、ヘラ付きピンセット、ハサミ、霧吹き

Materials You will need: *Leucobryum juniperoideum*, Miniature Cattleya, drift wood, 100% pure super glue cyanoacrylate adhesive, tweezers with a spatula, scissors, and sprayer.

10 Miniature Cattleya blooming on an old tree

1　流木にミニカトレアを置き位置を決めます。
2　ホソバオキナゴケを置き、付ける場所を決めます。ボンドを流木に塗ります。
3　ボンドを塗ったらホソバオキナゴケを置きます。コケの縁がボンドに付くようにします。
4　同様に3つのホソバオキナゴケを付けます。霧吹きをして湿らせると早くつきます。
5　ミニカトレアをポットから抜き、コケの中央に入れます。ミニカトレアが少し斜めになるようにするとナチュラルに見えます。
6　ホソバオキナゴケを根元に乗せてコケとコケをボンドで付けます。
7　いくつかコケを使い根元を覆います。継ぎ目が外れないようにボンドをつけます。
8　霧吹きをして湿らせ、ボンドを硬化させます。
9　コケの継ぎ目が外れないよう再度ボンドを付けます。
10　流木を回して位置を変えて、コケの継ぎ目にボンドを付けます。
11　霧吹きして湿らせ、ボンドを硬化させます。
12　ボンドが硬化したらシャワーでたっぷり水を与えて完成。
　3日に1回シャワーでたっぷり水を与えます。直射日光が当たらない明るい窓辺で管理します。

1. Place a miniature Cattleya on the driftwood and position it how you prefer.
2. Place *Leucobryum juniperoideum* and decide where to put it. Apply the adhesive to the driftwood.
3. Attach the moss and make sure the edges are well attached to the adhesive.
4. Place another 3 pieces of moss, and if you spray and moisturize them they will stick quickly.
5. Take out a miniature Cattleya from the pot and place it in the center of the moss. If you place Cattleya slightly diagonal, then it looks more natural.
6. Put *L. juniperoideum* on the foot of the plant, and attach the moss to each other using the adhesive.
7. Attach some more moss to cover the root with adhesive.
8. Spray water over the moss and wait until the adhesive dries completely.
9. Reattach the joint parts of moss with the adhesive.
10. Turn the driftwood around and attach the other joint.
11. Spray water again and wait until it's dry.
12. When the adhesive is completely dry, shower it and soak it.
Do this once every 3 days! Keep it by the windowsill, where it's bright but not in direct sunlight.

11 多肉植物とコケのアレンジ

多肉植物やサボテンなどといっしょにコケを植えても、
長期間栽培するのは無理です。
それは、本来の生えている環境があまりに違うためです。
しかしどうにかして、
いっしょに栽培したいと考えた植え方が、この方法です。

It is impossible to plant moss with succulents or cacti and keep them for long period, because they come from a totally different environment. However, this is the method of how to combine these plants together.

用意するもの シシゴケ、センペルビューム、硬質赤玉土小粒、石、砂利、ガラスの器、純度100パーセントのシアノアクリレート系ボンド、ヘラ付きピンセット、ハサミ、用土入れ

Materials You will need: *Brothera leana*, Sempervivum, red clay soil, stones, gravel, glass container, 100% pure super glue cyanoacrylate adhesive, tweezers with spatula, scissors, and soil container.

11 Succulents and Moss Arrangement

1　ガラスの器に硬質赤玉土小粒を入れます。
2　石を置きます。
3　センペルビュームをポットから抜き、用土を軽く落とします。
4　石の脇に置きます。
5　同様に石を置き、用土を軽く落としたセンペルビュームを置きます。
6　根元が隠れるまで硬質赤玉土小粒を敷きます。
7　センペルビュームの葉の下まで硬質赤玉土小粒を入れます。
8　硬質赤玉土小粒を入れ終わった状態。
9　コロコロとして可愛いシシゴケ。
10　シシゴケを付ける場所を決めます。
11　位置を決めておいたシシゴケを取り、コケを付ける石にボンドを塗ります。
12　ボンドは石の縁より内側に塗ります。
13　石に付きやすいように、あらかじめシシゴケの裏の仮根を濡らしておきます。ボンドを塗った石に乗せて押さえます。同様にすべてのコケを石に付けます。
14　砂利を全体に敷いていきます。
15　葉の下や、石との隙間にはピンセットで並べていきます。
16　軽くシャワーで濡らし完成。 明るい窓辺で管理します。シシゴケ やセンペルビュームに霧吹きで水を与えます。

1. Put the red clay soil into a glass container.
2. Place the stones.
3. Take out Sempervivum from the pot and lightly take off the soil.
4. Place it next to the stone.
5. Repeat the same process by placing a stone and putting Sempervivum next to it.
6. Cover the roots with red clay soil.
7. Add more red clay soil until it touches underneath the leaves of Sempervivum.
8. View after placing the red clay soil.
9. Prepare a cute and plump *Brothera leana*.
10. Decide where to put it.
11. Apply the adhesive to the stones, and place the moss.
12. It's better to apply the adhesive on the inside edges of the stones.
13. In advance, wet the back of the temporary root of *B.leana*. Place the moss and press it on the stone. Equally, do the same for all of the mosses.
14. Spread out the gravel.
15. Use tweezers to place the gravel in the areas under the leaves and in between the gaps of stones.
16. Moisturize with a light shower. Keep it by a bright windowsill, and water them with spray.

141

12 人研ぎ流しに作る苔の箱庭

用意するもの トヤマシノブゴケ、ハイゴケ、ベニチガヤ、ヒメヤバネススキ、カンスゲ、ナミキソウ、ソバナ、アオバナホタルブクロ、ミヤマウグイスカグラ、ヒメウツギ、イワヒバ、カタヒバ、溶岩、砂利、鉢底ネット、人研ぎ流し（じんとぎ：「人造石研ぎ出し」の略）、ヘラ付きピンセット、ハサミ

Materials You will need: *Thuidium kanedae*, *Hypnum plumaeforme*, *Imperata cylindrica Rubra*, dwarf variety of *Miscanthus sinensis*, *Carex morrowii*, *Scutellaria strigillosa*, *Adenophora remotiflora*, *Campanula punctata*, *Lonicera gracilipes* var. *gracilipes*, *Deutzia gracilis*, *Selaginella tamariscina*, *Selaginella moellendorffii*, copper-leaved *Deutzia crenata*, lava, gravel, pot screens, Japanese sink made by an artificial stone, tweezers with a spatula, and scissors.

12 Moss terrarium in Japanese Sink made by an artificial stone

1　人研ぎ流しのエンビ管落下パイプを取り外します。穴の上に大き目に切った鉢底ネットを敷きます。
2　鉢底ネットが動かないように、たっぷり砂利を敷き詰めます。
3　硬質赤玉土小粒を人研ぎ流し全体に入れます。
4　たっぷりと入れます。
5　溶岩を置きます。イワヒバやカタヒバの付いた溶岩も置きます。
6　溶岩を配置した状態。
7　枝ぶりが後ろから手前の角に流れるように、ミヤマウグイスカグラを植えます。
8　正面から見た状態。
9　ソバナをミヤマウグイスカグラの横に植えます。
10　もう1鉢ソバナを植えます。
11　左端後ろの角と溶岩との間にヒメヤバネススキを植えます。

1. Remove the pipe from the sink and place the sheet of the large pot screen.
2. Place a lot of gravel to make sure the pot screen won't move.
3. Put the red clay soil into the sink.
4. Use plenty of red clay soil.
5. Place the lava and other lavas with Selaginella tamariscina and *Selaginella moellendorffii*.
6. View after placing lavas.
7. Plant *Lonicera gracilipes var. gracilipes* as branches flow from the back to the front corner.
8. View from the front.
9. Plant *Adenophora remotiflora* next to *Lonicera gracilipes var. gracilipes*.
10. Plant another *Adenophora remotiflora*.
11. Plant *Miscanthus sinensis* next to the lava at the back left.

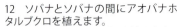

12　ソバナとソバナの間にアオバナホタルブクロを植えます。
13　右端後ろにベニチガヤを植えます。
14　少し植物を植えたら土を均します。
15　溶岩の縁にナミキソウを植えます。
16　もう1鉢並べてナミキソウを植えます。
17　クロバウツギをヒメヤバネススキの手前に植えます。
18　右手前に溶岩を置きます。
19　一度シャワーをかけて土をなじませます。
20　トヤマシノブゴケのシートを広げて持ち、人研ぎ流しの端に合わせて置きます。
21　溶岩の部分を指で裂き、溶岩がコケから出るようにします。
22　ヘラの裏面を使い、人研ぎ流しの縁にコケを入れ込みます。
23　全体にコケを広げていきます。

12. Between two *Adenophora remotiflora*, plant *Campanula punctatalam*.
13. Plant *Imperata cylindrica Rubra* at the back corner on the right　side.
14. After planting, level the soil.
15. On the edge of the lava, plant *Scutellaria strigillosa*.
16. Add another S. strigillosa next to the other one.
17. Plant copper-leaved *Deutzia crenata* in front of *Miscanthus sinensis' Zebrinus'*.
18. Place lava in the front right.
19. Shower the soil.
20. Take a sheet of *Thuidium kanedae* and spread it on the edge of the container.
21. Rip the moss with your finger to make the lava visible.
22. Use the spatula and press down the moss into the edge of the sink.
23. Cover the whole area with moss.

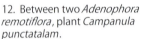

24 後ろのほうの植物の隙間にもコケを敷きます。
25 植物の周りはヘラの裏面を使いコケを入れ込みます。
26 溶岩の隙間にはハイゴケを入れ込みます。
27 ハイゴケはシートを片手で押さえ、使う分だけ引き裂いてシートから外します。ハサミで切るとバラバラになります。
28 すべての隙間にハイゴケを入れ込みます。
29 溶岩の上部にヒメウツギを追加し植えます。
30 ヒメウツギの左横にカンスゲを植えます。
31 植えた根元にもハイゴケを張ります。
32 裏側の溶岩と人研ぎ流しの隙間にもハイゴケを入れ込みます。
33 ハサミで枯れ枝を切り取ります。
34 細い枝は刃先が細いハサミを使い切り取ります。
35 何回かに分けて、シャワーでたっぷり水を与えて完成。
午前中日の当たる場所で管理します。乾きやすいためコケの表面が乾いてきたらたっぷり水を与えます。

24. Place the moss in the gaps of other plants.
25. Use the back of the spatula to press down the moss around the plant.
26. Plant *Hypnum plumaeforme* between the gaps of lava.
27. Use your hands to rip *H. plumaeforme* instead of using scissors, because it breaks down easily.
28. Put *H. plumaeforme* in all the gaps.
29. Plant *Deutzia gracilis* on the upper part of the lava.
30. Plant *Carex morrowii* right next to *Deutzia gracilis*.
31. Place *H. plumaeforme* on the foot of the roots.
32. Put *H. plumaeforme* in the gaps between the lava and the sink.
33. Cut off the dead branches.
34. Cut the skinny branches using thin bladed scissors.
35. Shower and soak it several times. Keep this terrarium under sunlight in the morning. When the surface of the moss is dry, give it plenty of water.

Column ❷

普通植物図譜
明治39年発行
村越三千男 画・高柳悦三郎 編・
牧野富太郎 校訂 博物学研究会 出版
この貴重な本の中で第1巻第11輯の次号予告にはスハマソウとゼニゴケがありますが実際の第1巻第12輯にはスハマソウの記載はなくゼニゴケの記載のみです。スハマソウ属の学名はHepatica。ゼニゴケ網の当時の学名は Hepatiacae。学名が似ているため、ゼニゴケだけが記載されのかもしれません。私はスハマソウもコケも、大好きですので、ゼニゴケだけでなくスハマソウも見たかったです。

著者所有。
From a collection of the author.

A Pictorial Book of General Plants
Printed in 1906
Illustrated by Michio Murakoshi
Edited by Etujiro Takayanagi
Compilation by Tomitaro Makino
Published by Natural History Study Group

In these precious series of books, particularly the volume 11 had noticed that they would publish *Hepatica* family and *Hepatiacae*(Liverworts) family in coming volume 12. However, it described only *Hepatiacae*. Since I am fascinated in both families, I would like to see the articles of Hepaticas. Maybe they misunderstood, as both families have similar names.

著者所有。
From a collection of the author.

James Sowerby

ジェームズ・サワビー（1751年-1822年）
植物学と貝類学の書物に、図を施してきた画家一家の始祖。
　1751年　ロンドンに生まれる。
　1765年　海洋画家リチャード・ライトのもとで修業。後に、博物画家ウィリアム・ホッジスの画房に移る。
　1777年　ロイヤル・アカデミー・オブ・アーツで、細密画を専門に学ぶ。
　1787年　ウィリアム・カーティスと契約。
　キュー王立植物園の機関誌『ボタニカル・マガジン』1～4巻の中の70図以上の作図 エドワード・スミス卿と『フローリスト・ディライト』（1789年-179年ロンドン刊行）、『イギリスのきのこ』（1797年-1803年ロンドン刊行）『エキゾティック・フローラ』（1804年-1805年）動物、植物、鉱物の分野で多くの博物図譜を編集した。
　またサワビーの名前が ヨーロッパオウギハクジラの英語名、Sowerby's Beaked Whale　キジカクシ科の植物の属名、Sowerbaea につけられている。
James Sowerby (1757~1822)

English Naturalist and Illustrator
The pioneer of the Sowerby family, who were illustrators for generations. They illustrated for the Botany and the Conchology.
Sowerby was born in London in 1765. He studied at the marine painter Richard Wright and later moved to the office of William Hodges (Natural History Illustration).
In 1777, he studied miniature paintings at the Royal Academy of Arts. He had a contract with William Curtis (Botanist and Entomologist) in 1787.
He illustrated more than 70 plates from no.1 to no.4 of the "Botanical Magazine" for the Kew Gardens.
He also published " Florist Delight" (1789,1790, London), " Mushrooms in England" (1797,1803 London) and " Exotic Flora" (1804,1805) together with Sir Edward Smith.
He edited many books about Zoology, Botany and Mineralogy.
Sowerby's Beaked Whale and Sowerbaea were named after his honour.

苔とは

What is Moss?

Weissia calcarea 1794年 ジェームズ・サワビー

苔の分類と体のしくみ

TYPE A 蘚類(せんるい) Bryopsida (Moss)

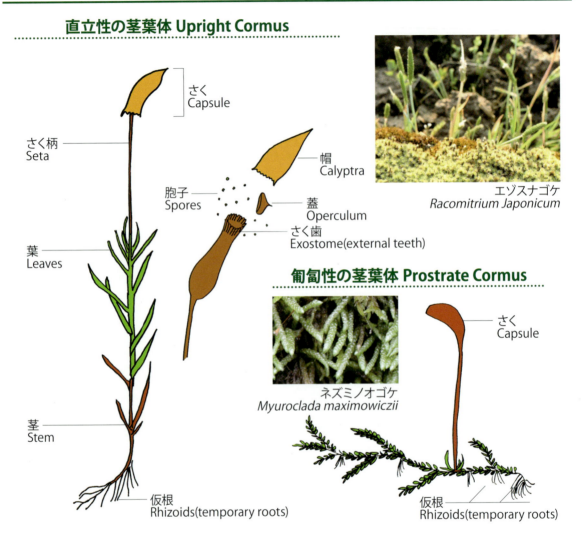

スギゴケ植物門(蘚類)

　蘚類は、茎葉体が直立性のものと匍匐性のものがあります。葉には1〜2本の中肋があり、葉は単細胞層で、仮根は多細胞です。造卵器や造精器は苞葉によって保護されています。直立性の蘚類は主茎の先端に1つの胞子体を付け、匍匐性の蘚類は主茎の途中に複数の胞子体を付けます。胞子体は、さく・さく柄・足からなり、成熟すると先端の蓋が外れ、さく歯が乾湿によって開閉運動を行い、長期間胞子を放出します。胞子での繁殖の他に、無性芽による無性繁殖や、茎や葉の一部が落ちてそれが再生し繁殖することもあります。

Bryopsida (Moss)

There are two types of Bryopsida: one is upright and another is prostrate. Their leaves have one or two midribs. Their foliage is single cell and temporary roots are multi-cells. The breeding organs are protected by bracts. Upright Bryopsida puts pores on the tip of the main stem. The prostrate puts several spores in the middle of stems. A sporophyte consists of a capsule, a seta and an axis. When it's matured, a spore case comes off and depending on if it is a wet or dry condition, external teeth (exostome) open to discharge spores for a long term. It also multiplies by the asexual bud and a part of stems and leaves.

Classification of mosses and the body structure

TYPE B 苔類(たいるい) Marchantiophyta (Liverworts)

葉状体 Thallus

茎葉体 Cormus

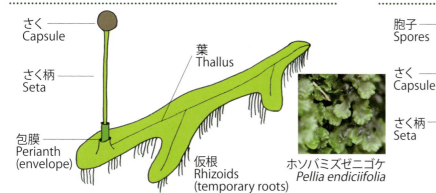

ホソバミズゼニゴケ *Pellia endiciifolia*

ゼニゴケ植物門（苔類）

苔類には茎葉体と葉状体があります。細胞に油体があり、仮根は単細胞です。葉状体の葉の腹面に粘液毛か腹鱗片があります。茎葉体の葉は2列の側葉と1列の腹葉が茎に付いています。胞子体は成熟するとさくの先端から4つに割れ、胞子を弾糸等で遠くに瞬時に飛ばし、枯れます。

Marchantiophyta (Liverworts)

Marchantiophyta have a cormus and a thallus. A cell has oil body and the temporary root is single cell. On the side of the thallus, there are sticky hairs or a ventral scale. The foliage of the cormus has two lines of lateral leaves and a line of underleaf. When a sporophyte matures, the capsule is divided into four. An elater immediately has spores dispersal and then withers.

TYPE C 角苔類(つのごけるい) Anthocerotophyta (Hornworts)

葉状体 Thallus

ニワツノゴケ *Phaeoceros laevis*

ツノゴケ植物門（ツノゴケ類）

葉状体で腹鱗片はありません。仮根は単細胞です。体には藍藻が共生しているときは青緑色に見えます。角状のさくの中心には軸柱があり、成熟すると先端から2つに裂け弾糸などで胞子を飛ばします。ツノゴケ類には、ピレノイドや分裂組織があります。

Anthocerotophyta (Hornworts)

Anthocerotophyta have no ventral scale and the temporary roots are single-cell. They look blue-green, when a cyanobacterias cohabitate. The center of the horn shaped capsule has an axis column. When it matures, it splits into two parts and the elater releases spores. Anthocerotophyta have a pyrenoid structure and a meristem.

149

苔のライフサイクル

スギゴケの仲間の例

　胞子が発芽し、緑色の糸状の原糸体を形成します。原糸体は成長し、茎葉体の芽を付けます。配偶体は、この茎葉体と原糸体から成り立っています。配偶体は成長して、茎の上に造精器と造卵器を作ります。成熟した造精器から精子が放出され水の力を利用して造卵器の卵に到達し受精します。受精卵は胚となり、造卵器の中で分裂を繰り返し、胞子体として成長します。成長した胞子体は先が膨らんで、図のような先端にさくのある苔の胞子体の形になります。このさくの中で減数分裂を行い、胞子を作ります。胞子が散布されると、また以上の繰り返しです。苔の胞子体は配偶体の上に共生して一生を終えます。苔は無性芽によっても増殖します。また、茎や葉などの一部が落ちても新しく茎葉体ができます。

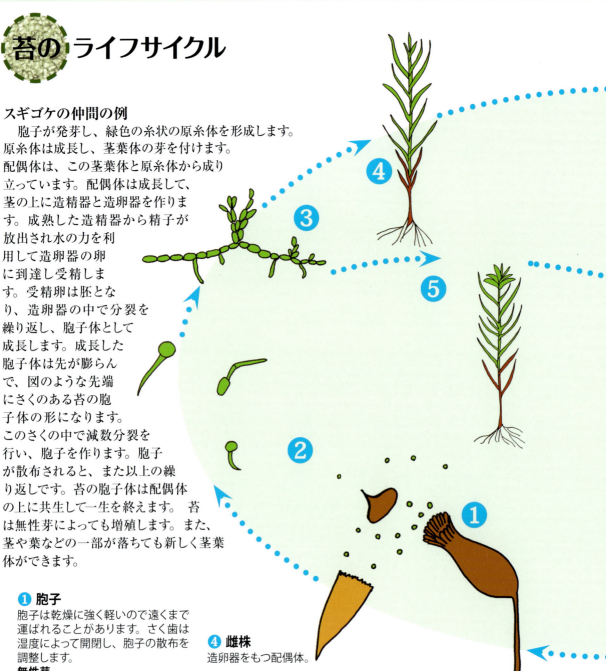

❶ 胞子
胞子は乾燥に強く軽いので遠くまで運ばれることがあります。さく歯は湿度によって開閉し、胞子の散布を調整します。
無性芽
蘚類では無性芽をよく形成します。無性芽から原糸体にならず、直接茎葉体になることもあります。

❷ 発芽
胞子が発芽し、細胞分裂を繰り返しながら原糸体となります。

❸ 原糸体
胞子が発芽してできる糸状の配偶体。成長して枝分かれし、茎葉体を形成します。一つの胞子からたくさんの茎葉体ができます。

❹ 雌株
造卵器をもつ配偶体。

❺ 雄株
雄株は雌株よりも小型で、先端に花葉が集まって付いた姿は花が咲いたようです。

❻ 造精器
雄株の上にある造精器。

❼ 精子
配偶体の上にある造精器で精子が作られます。精子が膜に包まれた精細胞が放出され、水の力で造卵器にたどり着きます。

❽ 受精
精子が水の中を泳いで卵にたどり着き受精します。受精すると胞子体の胚が形成されます。

❾ 胞子体
胞子体は成長とともに周りの袋状のものを破り、切り取られた上部のものは、帽となって胞子体の先端部を保護します。

Life cycle of mosses

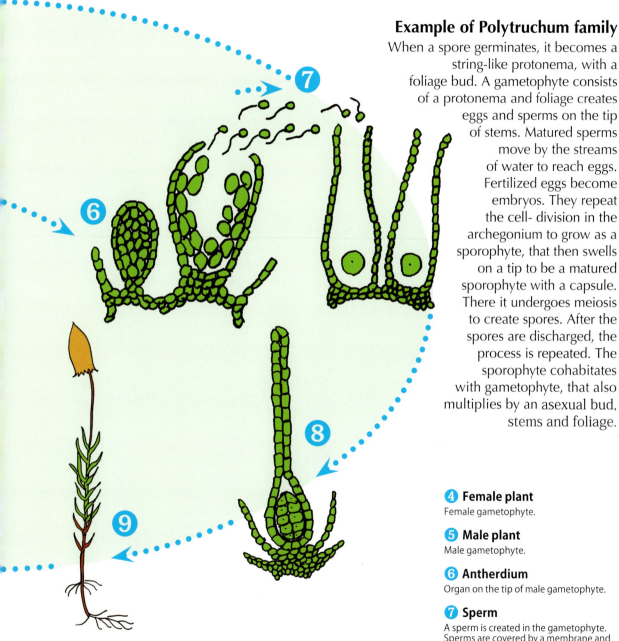

Example of Polytruchum family

When a spore germinates, it becomes a string-like protonema, with a foliage bud. A gametophyte consists of a protonema and foliage creates eggs and sperms on the tip of stems. Matured sperms move by the streams of water to reach eggs. Fertilized eggs become embryos. They repeat the cell- division in the archegonium to grow as a sporophyte, that then swells on a tip to be a matured sporophyte with a capsule. There it undergoes meiosis to create spores. After the spores are discharged, the process is repeated. The sporophyte cohabitates with gametophyte, that also multiplies by an asexual bud, stems and foliage.

❹ Female plant
Female gametophyte.

❺ Male plant
Male gametophyte.

❻ Antherdium
Organ on the tip of male gametophyte.

❼ Sperm
A sperm is created in the gametophyte. Sperms are covered by a membrane and move in the archegonium.

❽ Fertilization
Sperms swim in water to reach the egg. When it fertilizes, an embryo is created.

❾ Sporophyte
According to the growth, sporophyte brakes the bag-shaped things around, a part of it remains to protect as if a cap on top of sphorophyte.

❶ Spore
Since a spore is light and doesn't dehydrate easily, it can be carried far away.
Spores are discharged by external teeth (exostome) in response to the level of humidity in their surroundings
Asexual bud
Bryopsida has an asexual bud. It sometimes doesn't become a protonema, becomes foliage(cormus) immediately.

❷ Germination
When spores germinate and repeat cell division, they become raw threads (protonemata).

❸ Protonema
Astring-like gametophyte. When it grows, it branches out to have foliage (cormus). A spore develops into a lot of foliage.

151

苔のこと　　Current popularity of moss

最近は、街を歩くとガラスの器にコケを入れたコケリウムや、霧発生装置とともにコケのモニュメントが飾ってあるのを目にするようになりました。「コケ=暗くジメジメしたイメージ」から「コケ=可愛い、爽やか、お洒落」に変化してきたようです。コケは昔から庭に使われたり、盆栽や苔玉など、日本人の侘び寂びの世界にはなくてはならないものでした。時代を超えて人々を魅了するコケとはどんなものでしょうか。

苔は、水中から地上に上がった初めての植物と言われています。水の中では水不足の心配はありませんが、地上に上がると水の確保は容易ではありません。苔には根も維管束もクチクラ層もないので、水は体の表面から取り込むようになっています。そこで、乾燥に耐えるため、乾燥時には抵抗せず休眠し、雨が降ったら復活するという単純な方法で逞しく生きるようになったのでしょう。また、苔の体は粉砕して蒔くと、そこから新芽を吹いて増殖します。このようにして世界中のありとあらゆる場所に適応していったコケは世界中で約2万種類、日本だけでも約2千種類あると言われています。

以前はコケ植物門のなかに蘚類、苔類、ツノゴケ類が含まれていましたが、近年の分子系統学研究や、微細構造などの形態的特徴を元にした分類体系の再検討により、それぞれの分類群を独立した門に変更すべきという考え方が示され、スギゴケ植物門(Bryophyta)、ゼニゴケ植物門(Marchantiophyta)、ツノゴケ植物門(Anthocerotophyta)と、それぞれ独立した分類群として扱われています。この3つの分類群はすべてまとめて「コケ植物」と呼ばれていますが、遺伝解析の結果から側系統群(分類学的に単一でないグループ)であることが示されています。

学術的に観察したり、インテリアとして飾ったり、コケの風景の中に身を置いて癒されたり、それぞれの楽しみ方でコケを身近なものとして感じていただけたらと思います。

Recently, while walking on the street, I have come across moss terrariums of pretty glassware or moss monuments with a fog generator. Once, moss equaled dark and swampy plants. But it seems to be changing to cute, refreshing and stylish ones. For centuries Japanese have intensively used mosses: from moss gardening to bonsai and moss balls. They aimed to express rustic beauty with it. However, the charming mosses have become attractive for the new generations as something totally different.

It is said mosses are the first plants to come up on the ground from under the water. Although there is no problem in the water, it is not easy to keep moist themselves as mosses have no roots, no vascular bundles or cuticular layer. They take in the water from the surface. Therefore, it developed the system to be dormant in the dry condition. They revive immediately in the rain. If you smash mosses and scatter on the ground, they will emerge new sprouts. In such way, they grow everywhere. I can say it is the tough creatures. There are about 20000 species in the world. They say we have 2000 in Japan.

Once all the mosses were included in the Bryophyta. Recently they discovered new facts that they need to divide them into three categories. Bryophyta, Marchantiophyta and Anthocerotophyta. Although we call them all mosses, on the position of genetic analysis, they seemed more complex and different.

To research as a scholar, to decorate as an interior or to travel in the tranquil moss scenery for the therapeutic experience, there are so many ways for you to enjoy them.

撮影場所：ヨークカルチャーセンター小杉
写真モデル：真央さん

カルチャースクール

コケリウムは子供から大人まで大人気です。いろいろな種類のコケをガラスの器に入れ、小さなコケ庭を作ったり、コケと山野草などといっしょに植えた寄せ植えやコケ玉などを作ったり、簡単に自然に触れることができます。意外と子供たちのほうが作品作りが早いです。それは大人のようにいろいろ考え過ぎず、子供たちの柔軟な感性と直感で作るためではないでしょうか？斬新なデザインや色の組み合わせにいつも感心してしまいます。

開講教室
■ ヨークカルチャーセンター小杉
〒211-0063川崎市中原区小杉町3-420 イトーヨーカドー武蔵小杉駅前店5F TEL：044-711-8322

■ 相模原カルチャーセンター
〒252-0344 神奈川県相模原市南区古淵2-10-1 イオン相模原3F
TEL：042-776-3011

■ カルチャーセンター小田原
〒250-0872 神奈川県小田原市中里208 ダイナシティウエスト 4F
TEL：0465-46-1500

My Joyful surprise at Culture Centers
A moss terrarium to make your own is very popular for all the generations. A glassware moss terrarium, a miniature moss garden, a plant gathering with mosses or moss balls. Whatever you may create, it is the mini natural environment to touch and feel.

Surprisingly, children are easy going to make the art so quick. Maybe they are flexible and follow ones intuition, naturally. I am always surprised by their unique designs or vivid color coordination.

Photo: York Culture Center Kosugi
Model: Mao

Author's culure center
York Culture Center Kosugi
〒 211-0063 Ito Yokado Musasikosugi 5F 3-420 Kosugi-cho Nakaharaku Kawasaki City Kanagawa
tel: 044-711-8322
Sagamihara Culture Center
〒 252-0344 Ion Sagamihara 3F
2-10-1 Kobuchi Minamiku Sagamihara City Kanagawa
tel:042-776-3011
Culture Center Odawara
〒 250-0872 Daina City West 4F
208Nakazato Odawara City Kanagawa
tel:0465-46-1500

Q&A

Q1 苔の観察はいつがよいですか？

梅雨時期または秋の紅葉が深まる季節です。コケは一般に濡れている方ほうが綺麗です。雨の止んだ次の日は絶好の観察日和です。また雨のなかコケに付いた雫とともに観察したり撮影するのもよいです。写真機材が濡れないように注意しましょう。また山道では足元が滑りやすいので気をつけてくましょう。紅葉にコケの緑は似合います。北海道では梅雨がないぶん、春にサクラとコケの共演が見られて素敵です。

Q2 苔は殖やせますか？

成長が遅いため、時間はかかりますが殖やせます。育苗箱などに高質の赤玉土小粒やピートモスを敷き、葉、茎、仮根を細かく切ったものを撒き、たっぷり水を与えます。日陰で管理し、半年から2年ほどで全体を覆うくらいになります。

Q3 容器の中で栽培していた苔が伸びてしまいました。どのように手入れをしたらよいですか？

ハサミで伸びた葉や茎を切り取ります。少し短めに切るのがコツです。その時傷んだ個所があったらいっしょに切り、取り除きます。

Q4 旅行に行くとき、管理はどうしたらよいですか？

蓋が閉まる容器なら閉めて乾燥しないようにしてから出かけます。気温が高い季節は留守の間室温が上がるため、できるだけ涼しい場所に置くか、蓋が閉まる容器なら蓋を閉めて冷蔵庫に入れて管理します。ただし必ず凍結しない場所に入れます。水槽など大きな容器ではラップなどをかけて乾燥を防ぎます。

Q5 苔の葉先が白くなりました。どのようにしたらよいですか？

水を与えるのを忘れた時、葉先が白くなります。また、水道水のカルキやカルシウム成分により白くなります。その場合、白くなった部分をハサミで切り取ります。

Q6 水を与えるのを忘れてチリチリになりました。枯れてしまったのでしょうか？

コケは水分がなくなると休眠状態になります。霧吹きなどでたっぷり水を与えると葉が元のようになります。

Q7 苔が黄色くなりました。病気でしょうか？

冬、屋外で栽培しているコケは、種類によって紅葉し黄金色になります。トヤマシノブゴケやハイゴケなど。梅雨時期に黄色くなった場合は、クモノスカビや細菌によって傷んだためだと考えられるます。黄色くなった個所をハサミで切り取り、殺菌剤を散布して広がるのを防ぎます。

Q8 苔を購入するときの注意はありますか？

なるべく鮮やかな緑色で、チリチリになってないものを選びます。また、コケが入っているパックを裏から見て、枯葉や土、虫などのないものを選びます。山野から採取して販売しているショップもあるため、なるべく人工増殖した栽培品を買いましょう。

Q9 苔を採取することはできますか？

基本的にはできません。ほとんどのコケの生えている場所は国定公園や私有地の場合が多いためです。山の持ち主さんに許可を得てからの採取や、自分の敷地に自生したコケのみ採取しましょう。

Q10 庭に苔が生えています。コケリウムに使うことができますか？

種類によっては使うことができます。採取したら、コケに付いている枯葉や虫を取り除き、仮根に付いた土や砂利を綺麗に洗い、取り除きます。トレイなどにキッチンペーパーなどを敷き、水で濡らしその上に処理をしたコケを並べ、1週間ほど日陰で管理して枯れなかったら使用するほうがよいです。

Q1 When is the best time to observe mosses?

It is ideal to go and have a look them in the rainy season or autumn time, when the deciduous trees change the color of leaves.
The next day after the rain is the best timing. Also, it is nice to take photos in rain with rain droplets. But be very careful not to wet your camera. Since mountain paths are slippery, mind your step, please! Colored leaves and green mosses look very beautiful together. In Hokkaido, you can see the beauty of moss green with cherry blossoms.

Q2 Can I cultivate mosses?

Mosses are slow growers, therefore you need to be patient but it's possible. Put hard red clay soil or peat moss in the seedling raising box. Take foliage, stems and temporary roots and cut them finely. Scatter them on the soil and water thoroughly. Keep them in shade. They will grow to cover whole the box in half a year to two years time.

Q3 Mosses in the container elongated too much. How can I maintain them?

Cut off the longer leaves and stems to shorter size. Also, remove the damaged parts.

Q4 How can I take care of mosses, while I am away on a trip?

Put a lid on the container to prevent dryness. Keep it in a cool place. It's possible to put the container in a refrigerator. Please make sure you don't freeze them!
Put cling films on larger containers or tanks that you can't move.

Q5 Tips of the leaves became whitish! What should I do about it?.

When you forget to water, tips may become whitish. Otherwise it might have happened because of high levels of chlorine or calcium in the tap water. Cut off the white parts with scissors.

Q6 Since I forgot to water, the mosses became curly. Are they dead?

Mosses become dormant because of dehydration. Water them thoroughly with a damp spray. They may recover.

Q7 The mosses became yellow. Is it any kind of disease?

There is a kind of moss that changes color into gold in winter time. If Thuidium kanedae or Hypnum plumaeforme become yellowish in the rainy season, it could be rhizopus or any other germs that damaged the plants. Cut off the yellowish part with scissors and spray germicide to prevent disease.

Q8 What kind of moss should I look for?

Choose mosses that are vivid green and are not curly. And see underneath to check mold leaves or insects are not be in there. There are shops that harvest moss from the wild. However, it is better to buy from dealers who cultivate mosses, artificially.

Q9 Can I harvest a moss?

Basically, you can not. Almost the place, where mosses can be seen, is in the National Parks or a private property. You must ask the keeper of mountains or harvest only in your own property.

Q10 I have mosses in my garden. Can I make a moss terrarium with them?

It depends on what kind they are. Remove dead leaves or insects after you harvest. You must wash away the soil and gravels attached to the temporary roots, thoroughly. Place some paper towels on a tray, wet them and put the mosses on them. If the mosses won't whither in a week, you can use them.

苔管理・作業　　Management task

・置き場・
年間を通して直射日光と高温を避けます。
室内では明るい場所。屋外では主に日陰。

・ガラス容器や水槽での管理・
高温になる夏以外は蓋をして管理し、なるべく乾燥を防ぎます。夏は蒸れないよう、蓋をずらして空気が出入りしやすくします。

・山野草などといっしょに植えたコケリウムやテラリウムの管理・
秋から冬、室内での管理では暖房などで空気が乾燥するため、こまめに水を与えます。コケが乾燥すると直ぐにチリチリになってしまいます。

初夏から夏は、いっしょに植えた植物に応じて、朝陽が当たる場所か日陰で管理します。西陽は当たらないようにします。小さな器だと乾きやすいため、発泡スチロールやバットなどに水を張り、その上に置いて、周りの湿度を高めます。また、気化熱を利用して気温の上昇を防ぎます。

・コケのみをバットやパックケースでの管理・
梅雨時期に蒸れたり、クモノスカビにより枯れた場所は切り取り、殺菌剤を散布します。冬は氷点下になると霜によりコケが浮き上がりやすくなります。霜除けシートや新聞紙をかけて対処します。

・作業・
乾いたら、霧吹きまたはシャワーで水を与えます。コケの伸びた葉は、ハサミで少し短めにカットします。カビが生えたり枯れた場所は切り、取り除きます。いっしょに植えた植物の枯葉はカビの発生源になりやすいため、見つけしだい取り除きます。

苔の生産
コケの主な生産地は新潟県、神奈川県、栃木県、島根県です。林から自生しているコケを採取し生産したり、コケを細かくし、成長させて出荷するなど地域によって違います。新潟県の素心園では、コケの生産に稲作育苗バットを使い育成用土をバットに敷き、粉砕した種ゴケを蒔き半年から2年栽培し出荷しています。素心園で生産しているコケの種類は、スギゴケ、シッポゴケ、トヤマシノブゴケ、ハイゴケ、ホソバオキナゴケ、エゾスナゴケ、コツボゴケなどです。良質なコケを生産している素心園では種類ごとに、夏場気温が低く空中湿度のある用水路の斜面風通しのよい雑木林のなか、水持ちのよい田んぼの上など、栽培環境をコケに合わせ、極上のコケを育成しています。

育苗バットを手にする園主の三宮さん

Place to keep
Keep the mosses out of the direct sunshine all year long.
If you cultivate your mosses outdoors, it is preferable to keep them in the shade.

Management of glassware or water tanks
Except summer, keep the lid on to prevent dehydration. In summer, shift a lid a little for ventilation purposes.

Maintenance of the wild flower gathering with moss
From autumn to winter, keep watering indoor moss as an air conditioner makes the room dry. From early summer to midsummer, according to the plant's preference, set it on the place of morning sun or in shade. Don't put it in the place in the afternoon son! If the container is small, place it in the bigger container to keep in the waist water. It can keep the surrounding in moist and lower the temperature.

Moss in a flat tray or a strawberry pack
When they become damp or damaged by rhizopus in rainy season, cut off the damaged part and spray germicide. In winter, the frost make mosses rise up below the freezing point. Cover up with the frost free sheet or the newspaper.

Operation
When they dry, water by a damp spray or shower. Elongated foliage can be cut off in shorter by scissors. Molded part or dead part need to be cut off or remove. Since the dead leaves in a plant gathering may cause the mold. Remove them.

Moss production
Main producing areas in Japan are Niigata, Kanagawa, Tochigi, Shimane prefectures. Some companies harvest in the forest or others produce artificially by themselves.

Soshinen in Niigata prefecture, produces the moss artificially with the shallow tray for rice seedlings. They put the seedlings soil on a tray and scatter smashed mosses. It takes half to two years to grow and they make a sell them. They produce the best quality mosses. According to the preferable condition of mosses, they keep the tray on the slopes of the irrigation canals or in the mixed woodland of good ventilation or on the rice field, where the water can keep well. They produce *Polytrichum juniperinum, Dicranum nipponense, Thuidum nakedae, Hypnum plamaeforme, Leucobryum juniperoideum, Racomitrium japanicum, Plagiomnium acutum*.

Mr Sanguu the owner of "Soshinen" Garden holding the rice seedling tray

苔が見られる場所

群馬県草津町「志賀草津高原ルート」草津温泉観光協会
〒 377-1711 群馬県吾妻郡草津町草津 28 草津温泉バスターミナル 1F
TEL 0279-88-0800

群馬県中之条町「チャツボミゴケ公園」
〒 377-1701 群馬県吾妻郡中之条町入山字西山 13-3
TEL 0279-95-5111

群馬県吾妻郡嬬恋村「鬼押出し園」
〒 377-1593 群馬県吾妻郡嬬恋村鎌原 1053
TEL 0279-86-4141

神奈川県足柄下郡箱根町「箱根美術館」
〒 250-0408 神奈川県足柄下郡箱根町強羅 1300
TEL 0460-82-2623

長野県北佐久郡軽井沢町「白糸の滝」軽井沢観光会館
〒 389-0111 長野県北佐久郡軽井沢町長倉
TEL0267-42-5538

長野県北南佐久郡佐久穂町「白駒の池」佐久穂町観光協会
〒 384-0798 長野県佐久穂町大字畑 164 番地
TEL 0267-88-3956

石川県小松市日用町「叡智の杜 苔の里」
公益社団法人石川県観光連盟
〒 923-0324 石川県小松市日用町寅 71 番地
TEL 076-201-8110

石川県金沢市「兼六園」石川県金沢市兼六園 1-4 兼六園ガイド
TEL076-221-6453

岡山県新見市草間「羅生門ドリーネ」新見市役所産業部商工観光課
〒 718-8501 岡山県新見市新見 310-3
TEL 0867-72-6136

京都府京都市西京区「西芳寺」
〒 615-8286 京都府京都市西京区松尾神ケ谷町 56TEL 075-391-3631

....

イギリスのコケの観察地　England : where you can see mosses

ブラントウッド　Brantwood
The Brantwood Trust Coniston Cumbria LA21 8AD
enquiries@brantwood.org.uk
Telephone: 015394 41396 Fax: 015394 41263
http://www.brantwood.org.uk/

ゲートバローズ　Gait Barrows
Gait Barrows
Silverdale Carnforth LA5 0JF
http://www.naturalengland.org.uk

ニュービーブリッジ　Newby Bridge
Newby Bridge, Cumbria.
Newby Bridge Halt (also known, historically, as Newby Bridge Platform) is a
railway station on the Lakeside and Haverthwaite heritage railway.

シルバーデール　Silverdale, Lancashire
Silverdale, Lancashire
Silverdale is a village and civil parish within the City of Lancaster in
Lancashire, England.

Places where you can see mosses

" Shiga Kusatsu Highland route"
Kusatsu Town Gunma prefecture
Kusatsu Onsen Tourist association
Tel:0279-88-0800
Kusatsuonsen Bus Terminal 1F
28 Kusatsu town Agatsumagun Gunma
〒 377-1711

"Chatsubomigoke Park
Nakanojo Town Gunma
Tel:0279-95-5111
13-3 Nishiyama Aza Iriyama Nakanojo town
Agatsumagun Gunma
〒 377-1701

"Onioshidasien"
Adumagun Gunma
Tel:0279-86-4141
1053 Kamahara Tumagoimura Azumagun Gunma
〒 377-1593
1053 Kamahara Tsumagoimura Agatsumagun
Gunma
〒 377-1593

"Hakone Museum"
Hakone town Ashigarashimogun Kanagawa
Tel:0460-82-2623
1300 Gora Hakone Town Ashigarashimogun
Kanagawa
〒 250-0408

"Shiraitonotaki"
Karuizawa Town Sakugun Kanagawa
Karuizawa Tourist Association
Tel:0267-42-5538
Nagakura Karuizawa Town Kitasakugun Nagano
〒 389-0111

" Shirakomanoike" Sakuho Town Hokunan Sakugun
Nagano
Sakuho Tourist Association
Tel: 0267-88-3956
164 Banti Hata Ooaza Sakuho Town Sakugun Nagano
〒 384-0798

" Eichinomori Kokenosato"
Hiyou Town Komatu City Ishikawa Prefecture
Ishikawa Prefecture Tourist Association
Tel: 076-201-8110
71 Banti Tora Hiyou Town Komatu City Ishikawa
〒 923-0324

"Kenrokuen"
Kanazawa City Ishikawa Prefecture
Kenrokuen Guuide
Tel: 076-221-6453
1-4 Kenrokuen Kanazawa City Ishikawa

" Rashoumon Doriine" Kusama Niimi City Okayama
Prefecture Niimi City Municipal Office Commerce
and Tourist Division
Tel: 0867-72-6136
310-3 Niimi Niimi City Okayama
〒 718-8501

" Saihouji "
Nishikyoku Kyoto City Kyoto
Tel:075-391-3631
56 Kamigaya tyo Matsuo Saikyo Ku Kyoto City Kyoto
〒 615-8286

良質な苔の販売店ガイド
素心園
〒 949-4128 新潟県柏崎市西山町伊毛 1362-2 TEL：0257-47-3661
コケと雪割草を大自然の中で栽培し販売。
コケのインテリア コケリウム
〒 542-0062 大阪府大阪市中央区上本町西 4-1-9
ヴィレッジヒル上町台201　TEL：06-6763-0251 ※土、日、祝を除く
良質な苔などを豊富に取り扱う通販ショップ。

Good Quality Guide of the Moss Shop
Sosinen Tel: 0257-47-3661
1362-2 Imo Nishiyama Town Kasiwazaki City Niigata 〒 949-4128
They cultivate moss and Hepaticas in a great nature and distribute in
all Japan.
Koke no Interior Kokerium Tel: 06-6763-0251
201 Village Hill Uematidai 4-1-9 Kamihontyo Nishi Chuoku Osaka City
Osaka 〒 542-0062
*Open except Saturday, Sunday and National holiday
It is the mail order shop to deliver good quality mosses abundantly.

コケ図鑑索引

アップルモス	76
アラハシラガゴケ	69
ウェイブドシルクモス	80
ウマスギゴケ	48・73
エゾスナゴケ	49・72
オオカサゴケ	50
オーバーリーフペリア	80
オルトトリクム レイリア	77
カマサワゴケ	64
カモジゴケ	70
クジャクゴケ	51
クリーピングフィンガーワート	77
クロカワゴケ	65
コウヤノマンネングサ	60
コツボゴケ	52・68・73
コモンスムースキャップ	81
コモンタマリスクモス	78
コモンフェザーモス	79
コンプレスドゥエントドンモス	81
シシゴケ	54
シッポゴケ	71
ジャゴケ	55
スワンズネックタイムモス	75
スプレンディド フェザー モス	79
タマゴケ	56・72
ツルチョウチンゴケ	67
トヤマシノブゴケ	57・68・73
ナガバチヂレゴケ	63
ネズミノオゴケ	58・68
ハイゴケ	59・72
バンクヘアキャップ	74
ビッグシャギーモス	74
ヒノキゴケ	53・73
フラジル ケンフィロプス モス	78
ブライム モス	76
ホソバオキナゴケ	61・72
ホソバミズゼニゴケ	66
ホソホウオウゴケ	62・68
ラフストークトゥフェザーモス	75

ザオウスハマソウ
Hepatica nobilis var. *japonica* f. *zaoensis* Ohno&S.Tsuru.

156

Index

Atrichum undulatum	76・81
Bartramia pomiformis	56・72・76
Brachythecium rutabulum	75
Brothera leana	54
Campylopus fragilis	78
Climacium japonicum	60
Conocephalum conicum	55
Dicranum japonicum	71
Dicranum scoparium	70
Entodon challengeri	81
Fissidens grandifrons	62・68
Fontinalis antipyretica	65・69
Hylocomium splendens	79
Hypnum plumaeforme	59・72
Hypopterugium fauriei	51
Kindbergia praelonga	79
Lepidozia reptans	77
Leucobryum juniperoideum	61・72
Mnium hornum	75
Myuroclada maximowiczi	58・68
Ortotrikhum layelya	77
Pellia endiviifolia	66
Pellia epiphylla	80
Philonotis falcate	64
Plagiomnium acutum	52・68・73
Plagiomnium maximoviczii	67
Plagiothecium undulatum	80
Polytrichastrum formosum	74
Polytrichum commune	48・73
Ptychomitrium linearifolium	63
Racomitrium japonicum	49・72
Rhodobryum giganteum	50
Rhytidiadelphus triquetrus	74
Thuidium kanedae	57・68・73
Thuidium tamariscinum	78
Trachycystis microphylla	53・73

アシガラスハマソウ
Hepatica nobilis var. *japonica* f. *candida* Ohno

あとがき

本を書く時、何故かその前に素敵な出会いがあります。そして、『苔の本II』を執筆する時にも出会いがありました。 ここ何年か毎年春に、イギリスの、サクラや樹木の研究者であるRHSのクリス氏および友人達と共に日本の植物調査を行なっています。サクラやフジ、ツツジ、またシラネアオイなどの日本固有の山野草の調査です。

今年もその調査の途中能登に立ち寄りました。そのとき宿泊したホテルのロビーにあった本のな『旅するイングリッシュガーデン』横明美さんの著書があり、連絡をするとホテルの近くにプライベートガーデンがあるということで翌日訪れました。ホテルにその本がなかったらこの出会いはなかったと思います。今回、本書の企画段階で英訳付きにすると決めていたので、この偶然の出会いに感謝しています。

もう一人、素敵な出会いがありました。今回の本のデザイン構成をしていただいた佐々木達彦さんです。初めてのこの本の打ち合わせの時、本書の企画内容とイメージを話すとすぐに理解していただき、意気投合し素敵なデザインになりました。

また、野々口稔氏といっしょに行った2019ヘレボルス調査でも、調査隊の素敵な方々に出会えて感謝しております。

このように、たくさんの素敵な人に出会えるのは、母が川崎大師に頼み、私の名前を付けてくれたからかもしれません。母は私によく、好弘の名前は弘く好かれるようにと川崎大師さんが付けてくれたと言っていました。今、つくづく本当だなぁと思い感謝しています。

祖父からいろいろ動植物について教わり、興味を持ち続けてもう少しで半世紀になります。これからもたくさん研究し、新発見を発表できればと思います。

苔は世界中、いろいろな所に生えています。旅行先で、もし少しでも時間があったら地面や岩肌を見てみてください。きっと新たな苔ワールドが見つかり、時間を忘れて引き込まれることでしょう。そして、苔に興味を持ったら小さな蓋のある容器で、この本に載っているコケリウム用の苔を栽培してみましょう。栽培するときっと、苔の不思議をもっと感じられるでしょう。

苔は意外と環境の変化に強く、長生きします。使い捨てのインテリアにはしないで、可愛がってあげてください。

最後になりましたが、この本を読んでいただき本当にありがとうございます。

2019年8月9日 大野好弘

この本を執筆するにあたり大変お世話になりました
佐々木達彦さま 大野重子さま 横 明美さま Yukari さま
大出英子さま 谷道まやさま 倉田浩道さま 大原隆明さま
三宮順次さま 野々口稔さま 2019ヘレボルス調査団員のみなさま
Ms. Angela &Mr.Peter Unsworth Ms. Frances &
Mr.Adrian Garne Ms. Anne Porter Ms. Glenn & Mr.Dan
Shapiro Ms. Frances & Mr. George Whally Mr. Christopher
Sanders Mr. John Massey 中山一さま
たくさんのお力添え本当に感謝しております。
撮影協力 株式会社 カルチャー ヨークカルチャーセンター小杉
カルチャーセンター小田原

撮影
P112～P118、P120～P145 中山一
その他 大野好弘

参考文献 『フィールド図鑑 コケ』東海大学出版会・『野外観察ハンドブック 校庭のコケ』全国農村教育協会・『コケ図鑑』藤井久子 一般財団法人 家の光協会・『じっくり観察 特徴がわかる コケ図鑑』大石善隆 株式会社 ナツメ社・『Guide to mosses and liverworts of woodlands』Martin Godfrey FSC・『苔の本』大野好弘 株式会社 グラフィス・『コケを楽しむ庭づくり』大野好弘 株式会社 講談社

Postscript

Every time I write a new book, a wonderful encounter occurs.
For example, it happened, while I was working on "The World of Moss 2".
For several years I have been researching cherries, wisterias, azaleas or Glaucidium palmatum and Japanese native wild flowers together with my very dear friend Chris and his friends. Chris is a British researcher and a member of the RHS who specializes in cherries and trees. While working on the book I visited the Noto peninsula during spring and by chance I picked a titled " Traveling English Garden" written by Ms. Akemi Yoko. According to the book she had a private garden nearby. I immediately contacted her and made an appointment to visit her garden on the next day. I have never met her before but I wanted to have her translate my book from Japanese to English. I was very grateful for this chance encounter.
While working on this book, I also met Mr Tatuhiko Sasaki. Since the first time I met him I felt as though I found someone that shares many of my interests. He helped me make the book the way it is now.

I am also grateful of meeting with Mr Minoru Nonoguchi and his co-researchers at the 2019 Helleborus Commission . I always remember my mother used to say that my name was given from the Kawasaki Daishi to be loved by people. I felt that she was right, indeed. My grandfather taught me about animals and plants, when I was a young boy.
Because of that I have always kept enthusiasm and passion for nearly a quarter of a century. I still hope to discover new things, which may give people joyful surprises. Mosses are everywhere. If you have even a little bit of time, please look at the ground or at some rocks. If you ever become interested in mosses try starting….
With a little jar and a lid. You could discover a mysterious world.
Please remember that mosses will live for a long time, if you take good care of them. This doesn't have to be a short term experience.
Lastly, I thank you for taking an interest in my book!

9th August 2019   Yoshihiro Ohno

I deeply appreciate the contribution of Mr.Tatsuhiko Sasaki, Ms. Sigeko Ohno, Ms. Akemi Yoko, Ms.Yukari, Ms. Eiko Ooide, Ms. Maya Tanimichi, Mr. Hiromichi Kurata, Mr. Takaaki Oohara, Mr. Junji Sanguu, Mr. Minoru Nonoguchi 2019 Helleborus Commission. Ms.Angela & Mr.Peter Unsworth, Ms.Frances &Mr. Adrian Garne, Ms. Ann Porter, Ms. Glenn & Mr. Dan Shapiro, Ms. Francis & Mr.George Whally, Mr.Christopher Sanders, Mr. John Massey. Mr. Hajime Nakayama. Photography cooperation ; Culture York Culture Center, Kosugi Culture Center Odawara.

Photos:
春の "Peaceful Garden 岬の庭より"
能登半島の穴水町にあるイングリッシュコッテージガーデン。26年前に横清澄と明美夫妻がイギリスから帰国して作り始める。美しい内海に面した自然とアートと音楽が溢れる場所です。

This is the garden located by the inland sea of scenic Noto peninsula, Japan. Kiyosumi & Akemi Yoko have started to create an English style cottage garden after returning from Cornwall, England in 1993.

Photography:
P112-P118, P120-P145 Courtesy of Hajime Nakayama
Others by Yoshihiro Ohno

159

著者紹介
大野 好弘

園芸研究家1973年 神奈川県に生まれる。幼少より植物が身近にある環境にあり、さまざまな山野草やコケの育種を手掛け、とくに雪割草の育種研究は30年以上の経験を持つ。現在、世界の雪割草を研究するため、ワールドヘパティカラボラトリーを立ち上げ、大学との共同研究を行っている。中央アジアキルギスやヨーロッパのクロアチア、ボスニア・ヘルツェゴビナ、スロベニア、イタリア、イギリスでのコケや山野草、ヘパティカの調査をする。とくにイギリスには毎年行き、森の中で美しいコケの撮影を行う。また、ビンの中でコケを栽培しインテリアとして楽しむコケリウムの講師として、大学や各地のカルチャーセンターで活躍中。コケや山野草を配した庭のデザイン施工も行っている。そのほか、プロのアクアリストとして陰日性サンゴの研究を行い水槽内での累代飼育法を初めて確立した。イギリス人の植物学者と共に毎年日本でサクラやフジ、ツツジなどの調査を行う。 著書に『ザ・陰日性サンゴ』(誠文堂新光社)、『雪割草の世界』(エムピージェー)、『苔の本』(グラフィス)、『コケを楽しむ庭づくり』(講談社)がある。『NHK 趣味の園芸』では山野草の今月の管理・作業(2017年4月〜2019年3月)、『園芸JAPAN』では雪割草の世界」を今年15周年を迎え、好評連載中。テレビ東京系列 TV チャンピオン極〜 KIWAMI 〜「苔箱庭王選手権」審査員として出演。

イラスト：Yukari
英訳：横 明美　Peaceful Garden 岬の庭より 代表
撮影機材：Canon EOS 1DS mark Ⅲ
　　　　　EF100mm F2.8 マクロレンズ
　　　　　EF50mm F1.4

Author Profile:
Yoshihiro Ohno

Horticulture researcher, Agrochemical specialist, Chef
Born in Kanagawa Prefecture in 1973. From a young age, he was surrounded by plants and experienced cultivating wild flowers and mosses. Especially, he has been researching Hepaticas for more than 30 years. He set up the World Hepatica Laboratory and participates in a joint research with the university of Seikei. He went to Kyrgyzstan, Croatia, Bosnia –Herzegovina, Slovenia, Italy and England to research mosses, wild plants and Hepaticas. He goes to the UK every year to photograph beautiful mosses in the forest. British Botanists come to research with him about cherries, wisterias, azaleas and so on in Japan. Also, he is very much sought after as a famous lecturer of the moss terrarium in universities and culture centers. He designs and creates gardens of wild plants with mosses. He is also a professional aquarist, who invented a way to keep the deep-sea coral for successive breeding in a water tank, which was used to be impossible.
His other works:
"The Innichisei sango" (The Deep-sea Coral) Seibundo Shinkosha " Yukiwarisou no Sekai" (The world of Japanese Hepaticas) MPJ "Kokenohon" (The book of Moss) Graffice
"Kokewo tanosimu Niwazukuri" (Enjoy the Moss Gardening) Koudansha
Also, he contributes to many plants magazines. " NHK Syuminoengei" (about wild plants maintenance /April 2017~March 2019). For "Engei Japan" he has been writing about Hepaticas for 15 years and he is still writing.
Also, he appears on TV . He was a judge for the famous program of TV Tokyo "TVChampion Kiwami ~ Moss Miniature Garden Championship" .

Illustration　Yukari
English Translation Akemi Yoko 　Representative of "Peaceful Garden on the cape".
Photographic Equipment
Canon EOS 1DS mark Ⅲ
EF 100mm F2.8 macro lens　EF 50mm F1.4

苔の本 Ⅱ
2019年10月15日　初版発行
著　者　大野好弘
発 行 人　坂井雅之
発　　行　株式会社エスプレス・メディア出版
　　　　　〒108-0073 東京都港区三田1-1-15
　　　　　電話 03-5418-7735　FAX 03-5418-7736
発　　売　株式会社メディアパル
　　　　　〒162-8710 東京都新宿区東五軒町6番24号
　　　　　電話 03-5261-1171　FAX 03-3235-4645
印 刷 所　昭栄印刷株式会社

© 2019,Yoshihiro Ohno　Printed in Japan

ISBN978-4-8021-3171-1

万一、乱丁・落丁本の場合はお取り替えいたします。
本書の無断複写・複製・転載を禁じます。

Title: The World of Moss
　　　Illustrated guide book of Moss Terrariums and Gardening
By Yoshihiro Ohno

copyright © 2019 Yoshihiro Ohno
Printed in Japan
1st Edition published : 10th October 2019
Published by : Spressmedia publishing Co,.Ltd
〒 108-0073 1-1-15 Mita Minato-ku Tokyo
Tel: 03-5418-7735 Fax: 03-5418-7736
Release : Mediapal
〒 162-8710 6-24 Higashigokencho, Shinjuku-ku, Tokyo
Tel: 03-5261-1171 Fax: 03-3235-4645
Printing Works: Syoei printing Co,.Ltd

ISBN:978-4-8021-3171-1

All right reserved. No Part of this publication may be reproduced or transmitted in any form or by any means, electric or mechanical, including photocopy, recording or any information storage and retrieval systems, without permission in writing from the publisher.